O Come Emmanuel

O Come Emmanuel

AN ADVENT STUDY

ALEX THOMPSON

WIPF & STOCK · Eugene, Oregon

O COME EMMANUEL
An Advent Study

Wipf & Stock
An Imprint of Wipf and Stock Publishers
199 W. 8th Ave., Suite 3
Eugene, OR 97401

www.wipfandstock.com

PAPERBACK ISBN: 978-1-6667-3165-1
HARDCOVER ISBN: 978-1-6667-2434-9
EBOOK ISBN: 978-1-6667-2435-6

VERSION NUMBER 010422

For Beckett and Oliver
Rejoice, Emmanuel shall come to thee

Contents

Preface and Acknowledgments

Growing up in a small midwestern town in an even smaller United Methodist church, Advent didn't really mean anything to me. I could recall the Advent wreath, that circle of greenery with candles that we lit in December, but what it meant escaped my notice. The month of December was marked with too many other concerns: the constant shopping and wrapping of Christmas presents, the endless parade of special Christmas events and parties at school and church, and the regular cycle of family holiday traditions. Of course, the "reason for the season" was always squeezed into that crazed Christmas schedule. The church was there to remind us to remember the birth of Jesus. I assumed that Advent was a countdown till Christmas. After all, most of the Advent calendars sold in stores featured twenty-five days just like my family's countdown-till-Christmas calendar. That was the extent to which Advent was meaningful to me.

All of that changed for me during my first year in college. Through some strange circumstances, I found myself as a freshman college student in an upper-level class on Jesus and the Gospels. As I spent the semester reexamining my beliefs about God, Christianity, and my vocation in the world, this class opened up a whole new vista on the good news of Jesus Christ. I began to see how the story of Jesus' birth was not the start of a new story but the fulfillment and climax of a story already in progress. I learned how the story of God through the Old Testament formed the background for the story of the first Christmas. I learned that the story of Jesus did not begin with his birth in Bethlehem but on the first pages of Genesis. Many of these insights came through my close study of the Gospels in that college class. This initial excitement of understanding the New Testament in light of the Old Testament inspired me to continue to study the Bible in higher education for the next thirteen years. And it has continued to inspire me as a pastor and a professor to this day.

But this new reading of the Bible was also enlivened by new religious experiences. One of the many eye-opening moments of understanding Jesus' place in God's great story came at an Advent service. As the semester was slowly winding down and the air turned cold with the onset of winter, I attended my university's Service of Lessons and Carols. The old stone church was adorned with wreaths, evergreen trees, and the glow of candles. As the students slowly shuffled into the pews, a hush fell over the crowd as the university choir began: "O come, O come Emmanuel, and ransom captive Israel."

As verse after verse of the beautiful hymn washed over me, the threads of the Bible were knit together into a beautiful tapestry. The Advent hymn was speaking the language of the Old Testament, the longings and the hopes of the people of Israel, a prayer of expectation for the arrival of Jesus the Messiah. The hymn was all about understanding Jesus within Israel's story! Despite having heard the hymn before in church, I had never really understood its imagery until that moment. It was the combination of Advent, a close reading of Scripture, and this old hymn that opened my eyes to the significance of the gospel of Jesus Christ in a fresh way. Like the three numbers necessary for a combination lock, these three items worked together to unlock a greater depth to the story of Jesus.

Of course, this combination of the Christian year, Scripture, and hymnody is not an experience unique to me. For centuries, Christians have learned the good news and grown closer to God through singing, reading, preaching, and praying. But as the culture has become increasingly secular and some churches have begun to abandon their traditions for what is trendy and entertaining, this form of Christian formation has ebbed away. While there are signs that the tide is turning in churches with a return to Christian tradition, this book is my attempt to share in this process of revitalization through ancient practices.

My hope and prayer for this book is that it will invite you to a deeper engagement in this Christian tradition through song, Scripture, and the Advent season. The work is an Advent study that looks closely at the traditional Advent hymn "O Come, O Come Emmanuel." The hymns of the church are one of the ways that Christians learn the story of God. We sing God's great narrative of redemption in the language of Scripture when we sing the old hymns. "O Come, O Come Emmanuel" captures the sense of longing and expectation of the Advent season and gives us images and language that help us express the significance both of the birth of the Christ child and our world's continual longing for Christ's return.

The book is designed as a personal devotion or small-group study during the Advent season. It opens with a brief introduction to the liturgical year and the place of Advent in the cycle of the Christian seasons. Each of the remaining chapters will then focus on a verse of "O Come, O Come Emmanuel" with eyes toward the larger story of Scripture that the hymn reflects. The goal is that readers will learn the depth of God's great story contained in these short little verses in a way that will help them live more faithfully in the world. Each chapter concludes with discussion questions to help churches use this book as a small-group study.

This book would not have been possible without the support and encouragement from a number of persons. The initial idea for this book began years ago while I was a doctoral student at Emory University. The support of my colleagues, mentors, and professors in seminary and graduate school have grounded my work and served as an important conversation partner as I have grown in my vocation. Alongside the academic community, I am grateful to the congregations of Niota United Methodist Church and Cedar Springs United Methodist Church, who allowed me to test many of the ideas, stories, and explanations during the Advent seasons of 2019 and 2020. Many read early drafts of the book and encouraged me to seek publication. Special thanks to the folks of Wipf & Stock, especially Kara Barlow and Ian Creeger, who helped edit and prepare this work for publication. I am thankful for my colleagues at Tennessee Wesleyan University, especially Sean Hayden and William McDonald, who have served as excellent conversation partners and mentors through the publication process. I am also thankful for the many Holston conference clergy who have supported my work and ministry, especially Rev. Mark Flynn, who affirmed the quality of this book when I questioned it. I am grateful for the support of my family. I am blessed to have grown up in a great family—my parents and siblings have supported my faith journey through the years, even when I was unsure of the places I was going. Most of all, I am grateful for my wife, Mary, who has served as a constant source of support throughout the writing and publication process. She is not only a wonderful wife and mother to our two boys but also a powerful witness and minister of the gospel. She introduced me to the Jesse Tree, another Advent tradition, which has served as an important way we have tried to grow closer to God together as a family. This book is dedicated to our two boys, who I pray will grow closer to Christ throughout their lives.

Reader, may this work awaken your own Advent longing for Christ's return, even as you see in the child in a manger the fulfillment of God's great story for the world.

In Christ,

Rev. Dr. Alex Thompson

INTRODUCTION

Learning to Keep Time

How we talk about time often reveals important things about our society. Humans have always been fascinated with keeping track of time in various ways. The ancient rocks of Stonehenge, for example, were put in place to track the changing of the seasons. Similarly, for centuries farmers have structured their lives around a clear cycle of planting and harvesting with the seasons marking off the daily rhythm of life. More recently, the keeping of time has been shaped by new calendars. In Illinois every summer, I was bound to hear a farmer discuss his corn by noting it should "be knee-high by the Fourth of July." The farming season has now been supplemented by civic holidays on a social calendar. Farming is judged by the civic event of the Fourth of July. For most of my childhood, it was the school calendar that gave structure to my family's life. Vacations were predetermined by the dates for spring and fall breaks. The schedules of sports seasons often shaped the daily routine of the week. Football season was followed by basketball season just as fall gave way to winter. Spring brought with it track and baseball. There was a sort of rhythm that the school calendar gave to my life.

I still experience this rhythm every year as a college professor. The academic calendar gives a sense of expectation as the heat of August signals the return to school. There is a new energy and excitement that greets the start of each semester. But as the semester approaches its end with the onset of finals, a shift occurs on campus. As December rolls around, the colder weather matches the students' hunkering down to complete their final exams and papers. A somber and serious tone grips the school community. The arrival of spring, culminating in the end of school in May, is greeted with the joy and celebration reflected in the graduation ceremony. The academic calendar structures time at the university and creates a rhythm of life with its own accompanying emotions.

The church has long been aware of the importance of time in structuring life. Christians have their own calendar shaped by the life of Jesus. It is marked by the two most significant moments in the life of Jesus. Easter stands as the celebration of Jesus' resurrection from the dead. It is the day that changed the world because of God's raising of the Messiah to new life. The other significant day is Christmas, the birth of Jesus commemorated on December 25. Both celebrations are expressions of great joy and excitement in the church. These two dates are like the twelve and six on a clock. They split the cycle of every year into two halves. Around these two points, the church then adds other celebrations. There are days celebrating minor events in the life of Jesus, like Transfiguration Sunday, as well as more important days like Good Friday and Ash Wednesday.

But alongside these special days (the so-called "holidays" because they are *holy* days) are also seasons. Seasons are periods of celebration and preparation. Seasons often start or end with these special holy days. For instance, the celebration of Christmas on December 25 begins the season of Christmas (sometimes called Christmastide or Christmastime), a twelve-day season that ends on January 6th with the celebration of Epiphany. The church has a number of seasons that serve as extended periods of preparation or celebration around its holidays. The most well-known (even among non-Christians) is probably Lent. Lent is a forty-day season of preparation for the events of Jesus' death and resurrection. Lent begins with Ash Wednesday and culminates with Easter Sunday. As a season, Lent is a time of preparation usually marked by repentance and fasting. People give up things for Lent as a way to better grasp the nature of Jesus' sacrifice on the cross.

The focus of this book is one of these seasons of the Christian year: Advent. Advent is the first season of the Christian year and consists of the weeks leading up to Christmas. Advent usually spans three or four Sundays, with the actual number of days in Advent varying from twenty-two to twenty-eight, depending on the day of the week on which Christmas falls. Like Lent, Advent is a season of preparation. It sets the stage and the mood that culminates in Christmas. Coming as it does here in America with the colder winter weather and the longer nights, Advent has a somber yet expectant tone about it. Emotionally, Advent begins in the darkness and the cold. It begins with a longing. But it is also marked by hope and expectation. We light candles and watch for a new light to break into the world. Advent is a season of expectant waiting. In order to understand this tone of expectant waiting, we need to take a step back and understand the double vision of Advent.

THE DOUBLE VISION OF ADVENT

"Advent" is not a common word in the English language. It is derived from the Latin verb *advenire*, which means "to come or arrive." But "advent" does share the same root with a more common English word: "adventure." Yet Advent and adventure seem to communicate quite different ideas. Adventure immediately brings to mind exciting tales of near-death escapes, exotic places, and daring deeds. Adventure conjures up images of Indiana Jones in his jungle explorations as he avoids the booby traps of some long-forgotten civilization in order to get some precious artifact. Adventure is exciting and compelling. It keeps you on the edge of your seat.

The season of Advent, on the other hand, is marked by the lighting of candles around a wreath, the smell of evergreens, and somber music in a minor key. The tone is calm and decidedly unadventurous. Rarely is waiting seen as adventurous! But the overlap of the terms "advent" and "adventure" does give us insight into the meaning and significance of this season in the Christian calendar. Advent and adventure might have more in common than you think. Behind the traditions of candle lighting and somber music is a deep sense of expectation and anticipation. Advent is about a world that is watching closely to see what might happen. The adventure of Advent is about the anticipation of what God might do in the world.

In order to grasp that excitement and anticipation, you have to look behind the season to the hope that it represents. You have to understand how Advent operates on two different levels. Advent draws on two different stories at the same time. The first story is a story with which we are all deeply familiar. It is the story of Christmas. Advent is a period of expectation and preparation for Christmas with the arrival of the Messiah. During Advent, we hear the Old Testament longing for God to come and fix the broken world through the Messiah. In answer to these prayers and longings, God sends the Christ child to rescue the world. Advent draws deeply on the Old Testament stories of hope and longing. It gathers up the promises and expectations from the prophets and invokes a familiar cast of Old Testament characters: Abraham, Isaiah, and David. Like the final chapter in a good story, Advent offers the fulfillment of God's story in the Old Testament with the birth of the Messiah.

This means that in order to properly understand Advent as the preparation for the birth of Christ, one has to be deeply rooted in Israel's Scriptures, those books of the Old Testament. When the New Testament writers told the story of Jesus, they insisted that Jesus was the fulfillment of this bigger story stretching all the way back to Genesis. If we lose the plotline and language of the Old Testament, we lose the framework for understanding the importance and significance of Jesus' birth as the Messiah. Without the Old Testament, Advent expectation feels empty.

But Advent also draws on another story. Or rather, the second major act of the same story. For Advent is ultimately a story of *two* comings of Jesus. Just as the Old Testament prepares the way for the first coming of Jesus on Christmas morning, Advent also serves as a reminder that the church still waits for Christ's return in glory. We still await Jesus' return. Even after the victory he won through his birth, death, and resurrection, we still look expectantly for the complete fulfillment of all God's promises. We still long for the realized defeat of sin and death in the world. We still live in hope and expectation of the second coming of Christ.

Advent commemorates both of these stories at the same time and so creates a kind of double vision for the church. This double vision reminds me of the old 3D glasses I use to play with as a child. These 3D glasses had one eye covered in red film and the other in blue film. The way these 3D glasses work is that the images on the screen are depicted in two different shades, red and blue, to correspond to the different sides of the glasses. Your brain is given these two different images and, in trying to bring them together, makes the entire image appear to pop out of the screen. When you try to see two things at the same time, you end up with a dynamic single vision. The same is true for Advent: we anticipate the birth of Jesus even as we long for Christ's final return in victory. Red and blue images overlap in our minds. Two images, two comings, one Advent adventure.

TWO ROADBLOCKS TO CELEBRATING ADVENT

Advent celebrates both the first and second comings of Christ simultaneously. The effect, rather paradoxically, is that Advent appeals to contrary aspects of human existence as we live in obedience to the one true God. On one hand, Advent is a time of joyous expectation and anticipation of the celebration of Christ's coming into the world. But on the other hand, Advent also carries notes of longing, of a dream deferred and delayed, and of a cry of desperation for Christ's return in glory.

More often in our experience, Advent brims over with excitement as the church prepares to tell the mystery of its faith. As the Gospel of John explains the mystery, "the Word became flesh and dwelt among us" (John 1:14). Or, as the hymn by Charles Wesley exclaims, "veiled in flesh the Godhead see, hail incarnate Deity."[1] Advent is a celebration of the victory of our God, the God who was willing to become flesh to save us from sin and death. The light shines in the darkness. Indeed, churches often treat Advent primarily as a

1. *United Methodist Hymnal*, 240.

preparation for the Christmas season. Even as I was working on this book, I had a conversation with a well-respected pastor in my community about what his church was doing to celebrate the Advent season. He rather bluntly explained to me that his church doesn't really do Advent. Rather, Advent is always replaced by Christmas because he doesn't want his parishioners to go without hearing the good news of Jesus' coming. He explained to me that every Sunday is a Christmas even during the Advent season. He even gave me the following analogy. Having Christ is like having a gift that has already been opened. The surprise of Christmas has already been revealed with the birth of Jesus. You can't simply stuff the good news back into the box again! Trying to keep Advent as a period of expectation and anticipation for Christ's arrival is to miss that we have already received the good news!

But this way of thinking about Advent is misleading because it fails to take into account Advent's double vision. It neglects the element of "not yet," the future longing for Christ's return. Yes, there is a joy that comes with the Advent season because we know it will culminate in the birth of the Messiah. We know the Old Testament story will be fulfilled by the child in a manger. The church should not be afraid to share its good news. But there is something dangerous about overlooking Advent as a period of longing and expectation. For it fails to do justice to that other vision of Advent, the expectation of the second coming. After all, Christians still long for the return of Jesus. Over and over again, the New Testament calls for believers to "keep watch" and "be alert" for Christ's return in glory (Matt 25:13; Luke 21:36; 1 Thess 5:6). Even if we know the joy that comes with the arrival of Christ, we still expect Christ's return. To build on the analogy, if Christmas is like unwrapping the present, our current experience is realizing that the opened gift is only the first present of the day! Even as we have the joy of opening the first gift and learning of Christ's coming, so we are still looking forward to unwrapping the other presents as we live in expectation of his return. There is still an important longing, a habit of expectation and waiting, that we as Christians need to cultivate. Advent is a time to practice the waiting that is characteristic of the Christian life.

But there is more. By skipping over Advent and going straight into Christmas, Christians often fail to speak honestly about the darkness that still distorts the world. One only need turn on the TV to see the news of a world still deeply suffering under the chains of sin and death. The injustice of poverty still riddles our cities. Students go to school in fear of senseless acts of violence. Even the creation itself, this beautiful world, suffers under the weight of unchecked greed, pollution, and materialism. Our world groans for God's return. To avoid the longing of Advent and skip over the despair of the world in order to go straight to the good news avoids understanding the conditions of our world from which we seek salvation and restoration. Unless we acknowledge the depth of our brokenness, we cannot truly grasp the depth of the good news. We need the longing in order to live Christ's hope in a broken world.

The longing and sadness of the world is also present on a personal level. Every Advent, I minister to people in my church who will be spending their first Christmas without a loved one. In the past year, they have lost a grandparent, a husband or wife, or even a child. Christmas is not simply a time of joy and celebration. It is also marked by sorrow and sadness. That emotional weight is very real, and it is but a small slice of the sadness and sorrow that still grips the world. While Christ has come in the flesh and has rescued and redeemed the world through his death and resurrection, still we long for the fullness of this victory on earth. We must avoid the tendency of skipping over Advent's longing and going straight to Christmas.

Of course, the opposite is also true. We cannot get so bogged down in exploring the depths of evil and suffering in the world that we forget that Advent is also a time to lift our eyes up to the surprising actions of God. While the church must be aware of the depths of sin, Advent is a time not only to grapple with that reality but to pray and watch for God's deliverance. It is a time of *expectant* waiting. Advent should not turn all of us into pessimists who mope around with their heads to the ground and are unable to see God at work. Even as we pray and long in the darkness for the light, the church must keep its eyes open for the signs of light, truth, and life breaking forth. After all, the people who witnessed the arrival of Jesus the first time were those who were keeping watch. They were wise men looking at the stars. They were shepherds watching their flocks at night. They were Mary and Joseph, open to hearing the good news of the angelic messengers. Advent is a time to keep watch. It means being aware of the darkness around you but not letting the darkness define you. It means waiting for the light that breaks forth.

The church needs to keep Advent in its own way, aware of the double vision of the Advent season. A faithful celebration of Advent means gaining greater insight not only into the birth of Jesus as the fulfillment of Israel's story but also the role of the church as the people who wait, watch, and work in hope for his return in glory. This understanding of Advent is not some new development. It has been there for centuries as Christians have gathered together to pray, read, and wait before the celebration of Christmas. This beautiful and complex understanding of Advent is there in the songs we sing every year that weave together these two different stories simultaneously. One of these hymns, claiming a heritage that goes back hundreds of years, is "O Come, O Come Emmanuel."

O COME EMMANUEL

The story of the hymn "O Come, O Come Emmanuel" begins many centuries ago with celebrations of Advent in the eighth and ninth centuries CE among the monastic communities. In the seven days leading up to Christmas Eve, monks would gather together to sing the "O Antiphons." An antiphon is a short chant often sung in Christian songs, perhaps most equivalent to the refrain or chorus of a contemporary song. For the monks, an antiphon was often sung in response to a psalm in a worship service. The "O Antiphons" were written specifically in preparation for the Christmas celebration and thus capture the spirit of the Advent season. The "O Antiphons" serve as the template and inspiration for the hymn "O Come, O Come Emmanuel."

"O Come, O Come Emmanuel" was retranslated and recomposed in various ways over the following centuries, giving rise to the well-known version used in this book. Rooted in a long-standing

LEARNING TO KEEP TIME

Advent practice, the singing of the "O Antiphons" that make up the core of the hymn "O Come, O Come Emmanuel" goes back more than a thousand years and ties the longing of Christians of the twenty-first century to the longing of Christians of ages past. The hymn stands as a way for us to reclaim the celebration of Advent practiced by the church for centuries. It also offers us a striking example of the weaving together of the double vision of Advent informed by a range of images from the Old and New Testaments.

The core of the "O Antiphons" associate the birth of Jesus with various Old Testament images. I have included the titles ascribed to Jesus in the "O Antiphons" in their original Latin with explanations of their meanings below:

> *O Sapientia* (Wisdom)
> *O Adonai* (a Hebrew word for God/Lord)
> *O Radix Jesse* (Root or Stem of Jesse)
> *O Clavis David* (Key of David)
> *O Oriens* (Dayspring)
> *O Rex Gentium* (King of Gentiles)
> *O Emmanuel* (a Hebrew word meaning "God with us")

Each of these titles comes from the Old Testament and reflects the creative rereading of the Old Testament in light of the arrival of Jesus the Messiah. When one hears the Advent hymn, one is met with a dazzling array of Old Testament images that function almost like a mosaic used to depict Jesus. These images, like the season of Advent itself, have a kind of double vision about them. On one hand, the images draw from the Old Testament and point toward the ways that Jesus is understood as the fulfillment of the hopes and longings of Israel. For instance, to declare Jesus Emmanuel echoes the prophecy of Isa 7:14 and so follows a pattern seen at the birth of Jesus in Matthew's Gospel (Matt 1:23). But on the other hand, many of the images also reverberate with the church's ongoing longing for the return of the Messiah. To pray for Emmanuel to come is not only to echo Isaiah like Matthew's Gospel, but also to acknowledge that the church still longs for Christ's return as the people sent out with the promise that Jesus is with us (Matt 28:20). The "O Antiphons" are an imaginative masterpiece reflecting the double vision of Advent. The antiphons are like a suitcase stuffed with a range of clothes from across the Scriptures but which must be unpacked and unloaded to see all that it contains.

But there is more to the "O Antiphons" than meets the eye. Scholars have also noted that the first letters of these antiphons spell out *SARCORE*, which, when read backward, is *ERO CRAS*, a Latin expression that means "I will be present tomorrow." The very structure of the antiphons communicates a word puzzle that reflects the sense of expectation and anticipation of Christ's coming. While the order of the song as presented in modern hymnals has rearranged the verses so that this wordplay is lost ("O Come, O Come Emmanuel" usually comes first rather than last), the images alone still radiate with the double vision of Advent.[2]

"O Come, O Come Emmanuel" is a great example of the way that a Christian hymn helps structure a Christian understanding of time in light of the gospel of Jesus Christ. It invites us to locate ourselves in the Advent season, both in preparation of Christmas and in longing for the second coming of Christ. With each subsequent verse, we are invited to delve deeper into the mystery of Jesus and to let this shape our lives.

In the following chapters of this book, I invite you to join with me as we learn to keep time this Advent season with the hymn "O Come, O Come Emmanuel." Each of the following chapters will focus on one verse from this beautiful hymn. We will explore the Old Testament roots of these images as they point toward the birth of Jesus. But we will also consider the ways that these images of Jesus continue to reverberate through the New Testament as the church longs for Christ's return. Each chapter will seek to balance that double vision of Advent. We will rejoice with the story that points toward the arrival of Jesus even as we continue to long for and anticipate Christ's return in glory.

Advent is a season of waiting and expectation. Often, waiting and expectation is best done in groups, just as the monks centuries ago would gather together to sing the "O Antiphons." While this book can be read by individuals, I invite you to consider reading

2. For a brief discussion of the antiphons and their origin, Latin meanings, and arrangement into an order of worship, see Rutledge, *Advent*, 317–24.

it with a group of people. Use it as a small-group study in your local churches, workplaces, or even in your homes. Each chapter is designed to be engaged and discussed with others. Every chapter opens with a verse from the hymn as well as key passages from the Old and New Testaments that shine light on this image and are discussed in the chapter. Each chapter also ends with a series of questions meant to spur on discussion as you wait in expectation this Advent season. I invite you to join me on our Advent adventure together.

1

Emmanuel and Exile

O come, O come, Emmanuel
And ransom captive Israel
That mourns in lonely exile here
Until the Son of God appear.

Therefore the LORD himself will give you a sign. Look, the virgin
is with child and shall bear a son, and shall name him Im-
manuel. (Isa 7:14)

But just when he had resolved to do this, an angel of the Lord
appeared to him in a dream and said, "Joseph, son of David,
do not be afraid to take Mary as your wife, for the child
conceived in her is from the Holy Spirit. She will bear a son,
and you are to name him Jesus, for he will save his people from
their sins." All this took place to fulfill what had been spoken by
the Lord through the prophet: "Look, the virgin shall conceive
and bear a son, and they shall name him Emmanuel," which
means, "God is with us." (Matt 1:20–23)

LONGING IN EXILE

The Advent season does not begin with the birth of the Christ child in the small town of Bethlehem. It doesn't even start with Mary and Joseph and the surprising visit of the angels with news of great joy. Rather, Advent begins thousands of years earlier in the "lonely exile" of Israel.

Exile is a state or period of forced absence from one's homeland. In the twenty-first century, the term "exile" is often used in the context of political exiles, people who are forced to leave their homeland for various reasons. But in the Old Testament, the exile was not an event isolated to a small group of people. It was a defining moment for the whole Israelite community. The exile was one of the most significant events in the history of Israel and the formation of the Old Testament. Yet it is an event rarely discussed by pastors in sermons or in Sunday-school lessons. Nevertheless, our Advent hymn starts with it and so it marks the first stop on our Advent adventure.

The exile comes at the low point of Israel's history in the Old Testament. During the reign of the kings of Israel and Judah, the Israelites were prone to disobedience. Despite being the people of God, the Israelites had strayed from God. They worshiped other gods and neglected God's command to practice justice and righteousness. In response to this disobedience, God sent the prophets to call the people to repentance so that judgment might not come upon the nation. But despite the repeated pleas of the prophets, Israel and Judah persisted in their disobedience. God's response was to hand the Israelites over to exile.

In 722 BCE, the Northern Kingdom of Israel was conquered by the Assyrian Empire. In 587 BCE, the Southern Kingdom of Judah suffered a similar fate at the hands of the Babylonian Empire. The results of the exile were catastrophic for the people of God. The Israelites lost their homes and their family land. They lost their kings, those rulers whom God had promised would reign forever. The Babylonians destroyed the temple of God, where Israel encountered and worshiped God. To make matters worse, the Babylonians carted the Israelites off to a foreign land. All of the blessings of God had disappeared. God seemed to have abandoned the people.

The exile posed a significant challenge to Israel and their trust in God. Where was God in the midst of this? Could Israel's disobedience be forgiven and the exile reversed? The heartbreaking nature of the exile is captured beautifully in Ps 137, which opens with the following words: "By the rivers of Babylon we sat and wept, for there we remembered Zion" (Ps 137:1). Israel was left weeping by the rivers of a foreign land.

That image of the Israelites sitting in exile, weeping and longing for God to forgive them and restore them to their land, stands in the background of the first verse of "O Come, O Come Emmanuel." The hymn opens with the captive Israelites in lonely exile as they long for God to rescue them. The depth of exile is the start of the Advent story in this hymn.

The same shadow of the exile hangs over the beginning of the Gospels, though it often goes unnoticed. Perhaps the most obvious example comes in the genealogy of Matthew's Gospel. The birth of Jesus is traced through three sets of fourteen generations. The transitions between these three sets of fourteen generations in Jesus' family tree point toward significant moments in Israel's history. The genealogy begins with Abraham, the father of the nation of Israel, to whom God had promised to make a great nation for the blessing of the world. The next significant figure who opens the second set of fourteen is David. David was a king of Israel. God made a covenant with David that promised that someone from his family line would reign forever. Abraham and David make up the central promises of God to Israel for the sake of the transformation of the whole world. But then a dark shadow is introduced into the genealogy. The third turning point in Israel's history is the exile. The exile introduces the final set of fourteen generations. Despite all of the promises, the exile cuts through Israel's history and severs the people from their hopes. How can God's plan for the world come to pass when Israel has lost their land, their king, and their temple?

Matthew's Gospel continues from that exile for fourteen generations in a way that is also important. For although Israel's physical exile ended, there was a sense in which the exile continued for Israel even when they returned to their land. In 538 BCE, King Cyrus allowed the Israelites to return to their homeland from Babylon. The exile seemed to be over; God seemed to hear the cry of the people and let them return to the land promised to their forefathers. But the return from exile was hardly a world-changing moment for Israel. There was no Israelite king. Instead, Israel remained subservient to the Persians, who simply *allowed* them to return home. When Israel got to the land, there was not a glorious restoration. The temple had to be rebuilt, and once it was rebuilt, it lacked the glory and splendor of the former temple. As Ezra 3:12–13 explains, anyone who had seen the first temple wept during the consecration of its rebuilt replacement. It just wasn't the same. This could hardly be the fulfillment of God's promises. Even though Israel had returned from exile, exile continued to overshadow Israel's hopes. For fourteen generations after the exile, Israel waited and watched.

This is what Matthew's genealogy captures by placing Jesus' birth at the end of the generations of exile. In Jesus' birth, God was doing something new. God was finally going to reverse the devastation and destruction of the exile. The promises to Israel of a land, a king, and the blessing to the nations were finally going to be fulfilled. It is this hope that is reflected in the opening lyrics of "O Come, O Come Emmanuel." God had come to deliver Israel from lonely exile. But how would this return from exile be accomplished? The first verse of the hymn directs us to see the deliverance in the promise of the coming of Emmanuel.

SALVATION AND ISRAEL'S RANSOM

The exile of Israel was foundational for shaping the witness of the Old Testament. It acted like a magnet that attracted the various writings of the Israelite religion around a shared traumatic experience. The exile impacted the writing of the Psalms, as shown with the lament of Ps 137. The exile also left a mark on the earlier writings in the Pentateuch, those first five books of the Bible. For instance, Deut 29–30 warns that exile and destruction will accompany Israel if they fail to be obedient to the God of Israel. The exile was regularly a feature of concern for the prophets, many of whom warned of the exile. One can even read the story of Adam and Eve's expulsion of the garden after their disobedience to the command of God in Gen 3 as a story foreshadowing Israel's exile. Disobedience leads to expulsion and the loss of God's promises and presence. Exile is God's judgment. Such a theme left a deep mark on Israel's Scriptures.

Although the experience of exile was traumatic, it also gave rise to significant promises. Deuteronomy 30:4 declares: "Even if you are exiled to the ends of the world, from there the LORD your God will gather you, and from there he will bring you back." Similarly, many of the prophets who warned of Israel's impending exile also preached words of hope. They encouraged Israel that the exile would come to an end. God would act again to deliver and save Israel, and the promises of God's blessing to the world would still come to pass. Indeed, part of the disappointment with Israel's return from the exile under King Cyrus was that it failed to live up to these prophetic hopes. While the prophets looked for these hopes in their lifetime, the fulfillments often paled in comparison to the promises of the language itself.

The challenge of reading the Old Testament prophets is to capture the balance of fulfillment with the remaining excess that lacks fulfillment. The prophets often speak of events that would soon come to pass in their own day but use language that is so grand, so broad and beautiful, that the initial fulfillment seems to fall short of the prophet's vision itself. It might help to think about this using an analogy from personal experience. I can vividly remember the excitement and anticipation before a family trip to an amusement park as a child. The TV commercials about the joy and excitement of the amusement park were enthralling. I could envision how great the experience would be. I imagined the thrill of the roller coasters, the delicious taste of the sweets, and the overall satisfaction I would have on that vacation. The thought kept me up all night before we left. However, my actual experience of the amusement park fell short of my expectations. Yes, the rides were fun and the candy was sweet, but it fell short of the hype. The whole experience paled in comparison to my own hopes about it and the way it was presented in the commercials and flyers. Now, this failure of expectations could be addressed in two ways. I could simply acknowledge that the amusement park was overhyped and I was deceived. This is the case with most of our experiences. The reality often fails to live up to the hype. But there is another alternative. I could hold on to the hope that the next trip to the amusement park would be all I hoped it would be. Perhaps next time, what was lacking in my experience could be fulfilled.

It was that second choice that was consistently chosen by the people of God after the return from exile. The initial return from exile failed to live up to the expectations of the prophets. The glory of God was not present in the way they had anticipated. The coming king had not shown up. The nations were not flocking to know the God of Israel. Yet this was not because the prophets had lied or exaggerated. For the prophets were speaking the word of God. The truth was that the prophetic promises contained an excess of expectation that was yet to be fulfilled. There was a future fulfillment still to come. This contrast between the initial fulfillment and the hope for total fulfillment will be helpful in understanding Jesus in relation to the prophetic promises of the Old Testament.

With this framework in mind, let us return to "O Come, O Come Emmanuel," as the first verse invokes Matthew's Gospel and the promise of Emmanuel. In Matt 1, Joseph has just heard that his wife-to-be, Mary, is pregnant. This is quite the scandal, and Joseph, being righteous, has decided to dismiss her quietly. But just as he has resolved to do this, an angel of the Lord appears to him in a dream. The angel tells him that this child born of Mary is from the Holy Spirit. The angel then goes on to tell Joseph what the name of this child should be using several important terms.

First, the angel explains that he will be named Jesus, for the child will save his people from their sins. The name Jesus is derived from the Hebrew *Yeshua*, which means "to save." It is related to the name Joshua. The most famous Joshua was the Israelite leader who led the people into the promised land. Jesus will bear this name because he too will save the people. Jesus will bring the promised salvation of his people. Yet it will not be Joshua's military salvation but a salvation from sins (Matt 1:21).

But what does salvation from sins mean for the earliest Christians? In the wake of the evangelical movements in America in the mid-twentieth century, the language of salvation and "being saved" has become quite common in Christian circles. I grew up with the language of being "saved." The church I attended in high school often stressed salvation, with students wearing it as a badge of honor in youth group. But salvation was defined in a specific way. It meant coming down to the altar, confessing your sins, and receiving Jesus into your heart. Jesus saved you from your sins, just as Matthew's Gospel had promised. Now, there is nothing wrong with this language of personal salvation. But when we focus on this "personal salvation," we often misunderstand the significance of Jesus' birth in its ancient context. Salvation from sins in Jesus' day was tightly connected to the language of exile. For, as Matthew explains, Jesus came to "save *his people from their sins.*" (Matt 1:21, italics added). His people, of course, being the Jewish people, whose sins had landed them in exile.

This language of salvation has a special significance in light of Israel's exile. The exile of Israel was a result of their disobedience and their sinfulness. They had abandoned the worship of God for idols. They had failed to practice the justice and righteousness required by the law. They had sinned against the Lord. The exile was the result of their sins. That meant that an end to exile would require the forgiveness of sins and a deliverance from sinfulness and the exile such sinfulness produced. The prophet Isaiah declares that the end of exile would mean "that [Israel] has served her term, that her penalty is paid, that she has received from the LORD's hand double for all her sins" (Isa 40:2). Forgiveness of sins and salvation were connected to the end of exile. It was a hope for the whole people of Israel, who longed for God's salvation.

This Old Testament imagery of salvation was shaped by the most important event of Israel's history: the exodus. The exodus was the moment God acted in history to deliver the Israelites from slavery. God freed the captives from slavery and brought them out to a land flowing with milk and honey. The exodus was described in several different ways. One of those terms was "ransom," meaning the price paid for freedom secured. The basic idea is that God purchased Israel's freedom from Egyptian oppression. Israel was ransomed from Egypt by God's mighty acts of salvation. Salvation won their freedom. The prophets often reused the language of ransom and salvation as it was shaped by the exodus to describe the return from exile (e.g., Isa 45:13). After all, if God had acted once to deliver Israel from a foreign land and foreign oppression, God could act again to reverse their fortunes.

But how does that language of salvation fit with the emphasis on personal salvation so common in the church? What was revealed by the exile was a deeper awareness of the depth of Israel's own brokenness. Individual and communal sin were wrapped up together. The reason for the exile was Israel's own disobedience, both individually and collectively. Israel had learned that God needed to deliver them from slavery in a foreign land and the slavery to their own sinfulness and disobedience. After all, the exile was the result of Israel's own shortcomings. The exile helped the language of salvation become much more complex. Israel needed saving from powers outside themselves as well as powers within themselves. God has to fix the individuals and the world. The personal and communal are wrapped up together. All of this stands in the background of that line from "O Come, O Come Emmanuel" which says that the coming Messiah will "ransom captive Israel." Israel, in exile and sinfulness, needs salvation and forgiveness. There must be a ransom.

This richer understanding of salvation in Israel's scriptures helps us understand what exile means for us today. We, like Israel, know what it is like to sit in exile whenever we long for God's promises to be fulfilled in our midst. We have sat by the bed of loved ones slowly passing away. We have sat with tears in our eyes watching the news of atrocities on TV, such as terrorist attacks and school shootings. We have seen the people on the side of the road sitting in poverty as a testament to a world that is still broken. But we also know exile as a result of our own personal sin. We know the depth of our brokenness expressed in the words of hate we utter against others or the tendencies in our own heart toward greed, lust, and injustice. The world is broken by injustice, and we are broken by sinfulness. Our cry for salvation and redemption resounds with the cry of the Israelites in exile. As the cry of the hymn expresses, we need God to come and "ransom captive Israel." To redeem those who are enslaved to themselves, to the evil forces of the world, and to things not of God. We are captive and long for deliverance and freedom. In response to this language of exile and sin, the promised Messiah emerged. Jesus will deliver us from our sins. But that is only the first name the angel gives. There is still another, more shocking, name that will follow.

EMMANUEL, GOD WITH US

Up to this point, we have seen how the promise of Jesus' birth to Joseph is understood as bringing an end to Israel's plight of exile. Jesus will come to save the people from their sins with a great new exodus. But that is not the end of the passage from Matt 1 or the end of the story invoked by the first stanza of "O Come, O Come Emmanuel." For as Matt 1 continues, we learn of another name that will be given to this child. As Matthew's Gospel explains, "All this took place to fulfill what had been spoken by the Lord through the prophet: 'Look, the virgin shall conceive and bear a son, and they shall name him Emmanuel,' which means God with us" (Matt 1:22–23).

Here we learn of the origin of the name Emmanuel, which hangs over the entire hymn. As Scripture explains, Emmanuel means "God with us" and has its start in an oracle of the prophet Isaiah. Before the exile, King Ahaz of Judah feared the threat of destruction by a number of warring nations that appeared to be planning to attack Jerusalem. Dreading the overthrow of his kingdom and the loss of God's promises, Ahaz was scared of an impending exile. But Isaiah the prophet showed up and said that God would give Ahaz a sign that God would not abandon the people into the hands of the enemy. A young woman was with child who would be named Emmanuel (Isa 7:14). The oracle goes on to explain that before the child grew too old, Ahaz would see his enemies defeated (7:15–16). A close reading of Isa 7 reveals that the original setting of this prophetic message was given to Ahaz prior to the exile. It was a word of hope. The term later translated as "virgin" in Matt 1 can also just mean "maiden" or "young woman" in Hebrew, giving the passage a less remarkable tone. The general sense of the prophet's message was that the birth of a child either to the prophet's wife or to one of Ahaz's wives would be a confirmation that God would deliver Ahaz. There is little surprise in the oracle initially. Elsewhere in Isaiah, we see children given symbolic names meant to communicate a message to the people (cf. Isa 8:1–4). The oracle had a meaning for Ahaz in his own day and time that was clear.

But as is the case with prophetic oracles, there was also an excess of meaning that pointed toward an even greater future. For the earliest Christians, that excess of meaning was in the translation of the Hebrew word for maiden to the Greek word for virgin. The child born would not be an ordinary child. It would come by extraordinary means. The birth of Jesus to the virgin Mary was taken as the total fulfillment of this oracle of Isaiah the prophet. Through the birth of this child, the exile would come to an end, Israel's sins would be forgiven, and God would fix what was broken with the world.

The brilliance of that hope is imbedded in the name Emmanuel, God with us. For ancient Israel, God's primary presence with the people was in the temple. The temple was God's dwelling place on earth. With the Babylonian exile, the temple was destroyed and God's presence departed from Israel. But even with the rebuilt temple after the exile, the glory had not returned. There was still the longing for God's return to the people. Yet, in the birth of Jesus, in fulfillment of this oracle from Isaiah, God promised to be with the people again. In Jesus, God was coming. As the angel explains in Matt 1, Jesus is Emmanuel, the God who is with the people. A new age was dawning. The exile ends when the Son of God appears.

Matthew's Gospel makes this point explicit both at the end and at the beginning of its narrative. Here at his birth, Jesus is said to be God's presence with the people. After his death and resurrection, Jesus again reminds the disciples of this promise. In Matt 28, Jesus equips the disciples with the new task of making disciples throughout the world. As the sign of encouragement and reassurance for this task, Jesus reminds them of his name Emmanuel when he explains, "I am with you always, to the end of the age" (Matt 28:20). God has come in Jesus. God will be with the church through Jesus. Jesus' arrival reverses Israel's exile, brings salvation from sins, and is God's very presence with the people.

Despite all that is broken in the world, God has brought salvation in Jesus, and Jesus will return to make all things new. Just as Israel cries out from exile for God to redeem, so we as the church cry out for Christ to return. In response, Jesus reminds us that he is with us. God is with us in Jesus. Emmanuel provides a beautiful link not only to the mystery of the manger but also to the longing of the church for his return in glory.

CONCLUSION

The first verse of "O Come, O Come Emmanuel" sets the stage for understanding Advent by locating Jesus in Israel's story. It invokes the exile and the hope for God's return, the language of sin and ransom, and the promise of God's presence. It serves as a reminder that preparation for the Christmas season is part of a larger story of God's unfailing love and commitment to Israel and to the whole world. It is the story and language of the Old Testament that is the necessary framework for understanding the arrival of the Christ child. To read the Gospels without this Old Testament framework is like walking in on a movie ten minutes before the end. The characters and plot won't make sense. But if we take Advent seriously, we are invited to prepare ourselves for the miracle of Christmas by hearing again the broader story. "O Come, O Come Emmanuel" shows us what this looks like. It serves as an invitation to see in the child in a manger the fulfillment of a wider story of God's purposes for the world. The first verse starts us on this adventure, and the subsequent verses will offer us further directions that point the way to the manger and, beyond it, to the second coming of Christ.

DISCUSSION QUESTIONS FOR CHAPTER 1

1. What does exile mean? Have you ever heard exile preached or taught in your church? How does exile shape the Old Testament and prepare for Jesus' arrival?
2. Can you think of an experience that failed to live up to expectations? How did you respond? How does this experience compare to Advent?
3. What does salvation mean in your experience? How is that different from salvation as presented in the Old Testament and the start of Matthew's Gospel?
4. Can you think of a personal sin that separates you from God? Can you think of a sinful structure in the world that reveals the brokenness of creation?
5. What does it mean for Jesus to be Emmanuel for you in the church today? Where is Jesus present with you?
6. What is one way that you could remember and reflect on exile and Emmanuel this Advent season?

2

Wisdom and the Word

O come, O Wisdom from on high
Who ordered all things mightily,
To us the path of knowledge show
And cause us in its ways to go.

[Wisdom says,] The LORD *created me at the beginning of his*
work, the first of his acts of long ago. Ages ago I was set up, at
the first, before the beginning of the earth. When there were
no depths I was brought forth, when there were no springs
abounding with water . . . when he assigned to the sea its limit,
so that the waters might not transgress his command, when
he marked out the foundations of the earth, then I was beside
him, like a master worker; and I was daily his delight, rejoic-
ing before him always, rejoicing in his inhabited world and
delighting in the human race. (Prov 8:22–24, 29–31)

In the beginning was the Word, and the Word was with God,
and the Word was God. He was in the beginning with God. All
things came into being through him, and without him not one
thing came into being. What has come into being in him was
life, and the life was the light of all people. The light shines in

the darkness, and the darkness did not overcome it. . . . And
the Word became flesh and lived among us, and we have seen
his glory, the glory as of a father's only son, full of grace and
truth. (John 1:15, 14)

WHERE CAN WISDOM BE FOUND?

"Just because you are college educated doesn't mean that you are
wise." As someone who was in college for more than a decade, there
has been more than a few times I've heard this statement. More
often than not, it happened in the small hometown where I grew
up as I returned home for the holidays to catch up with old friends,
visit with my family, and attend the church that raised me. Many
of those in my hometown who did not attend college are quick to
remind me that college doesn't make one wise. Sure, you get to read
lots of books and take classes. But there is a difference between getting smart and being wise. There are lots of smart people who have
earned degrees who can't change a tire, maintain a garden, or cook
a decent meal. Reading books doesn't equip you with the ability
to say the right words to people in need, offer advice to someone
struggling with a traumatic loss, or guide a troubled youth off a
path leading to destruction. Those things require wisdom, and
wisdom is often gained from years of life experience. For those in
the church, wisdom comes from a life lived intentionally in obedience to God and Christ, a willingness to continue to grow and learn
despite whatever hardships life throws at you. Eugene Peterson's
description of discipleship is equally as fitting a description of wisdom: it is "a long obedience in a single direction."[1]

Of course, it is not just we in the modern world who show a
deep concern for wisdom. Wisdom has been a hallmark of civilization. It was passed down in sayings from parents to their children
just as parents today instruct their kids. Wisdom was passed down
in schools, whether to students who gathered around a Greek phi-
losopher or disciples who followed a Jewish rabbi. Wisdom was
also a crucial part of government. Kings often had official "wise

1. Peterson, *Long Obedience*, 17.

men" who would advise them on affairs of the state. Cultures as different as the Chinese or the Egyptians all had their sages that would dispense advice. The quest for wisdom is universal, though not everyone agrees on what counts as wisdom. Still, people have for millennia insisted that there are wise ways of living in the world and there are foolish ways.

Wisdom has also left a significant mark on the Bible. In the Old Testament, there are a number of books of wisdom that articulate how best to live wisely in the world. One example is the book of Proverbs. Proverbs is shaped as a transmission of wise advice from parents to their children. Proverbs 1:8 exhorts the reader to "heed, my child, your father's instruction, and do not reject your mother's teaching." In the unfolding chapters of Proverbs, the reader is given a series of short sayings on how to choose wisdom and reject foolishness. Standing at the front of this instruction is a proverb that reminds the reader that wisdom is ultimately rooted in God: "The fear of the LORD is the beginning of knowledge" (Prov 1:7a). For the ancient Israelites, all wisdom is traced back to God. A quick perusal of the rest of the Old Testament would confirm this point, as Proverbs comes alongside other, quite different books of wisdom, like Ecclesiastes or Job. The quest for wisdom was one of the ways that Israel sought to be faithful to their God. For the Israelites, learning wisdom meant drawing close to the God who gave order to the world around them.

And yet, one of the fascinating things about the Old Testament wisdom books is that wisdom is not limited to the special knowledge of the Israelites. Proverbs is willing to borrow wisdom from a range of sources and cultures. There are wisdom sayings taken from the Egyptians and other ancient Near Eastern civilizations. There are collections of sayings from King Lemuel's mother and the words of Agur (Prov 30–31). This shows us that wisdom in ancient Israel was remarkably open to the rest of the world. But this makes sense for the Israelites. After all, if someone is truly wise, they are not just wise in the eyes of their own people. Their wisdom should be apparent to the whole world, as the one God is the source of all wisdom. Perhaps even the non-Israelites had insights that could help the Israelites better worship and understand their God.

It is into this world of wisdom that the second verse of "O Come, O Come Emmanuel" takes us. Jesus is celebrated as "Wisdom from on high" that comes to show humanity the paths of knowledge. In order to understand this verse, one has to dive deep into Israel's understanding of wisdom, its relation to God, and the ordering of the whole universe.

WISDOM, CREATION, AND THE WORD

Israel's quest for wisdom doesn't begin with the book of Proverbs. Its roots actually go back to the creation of the world. For Israel (as for many of ancient cultures), wisdom was rooted in understanding the very order and purpose of creation. Wisdom meant understanding that the world and the relationship of all of the things in it were there for a reason. The world was not simply a chaotic mess. There was order to the world as shaped by God. The quest for wisdom meant seeking out and uncovering this order. Israel's understanding of wisdom has its roots in creation and in the God who created all things.

The book of Genesis opens over a vast nothingness, a kind of sea of unformed watery mess, a "formless void" (Gen 1:2). But over this chaos is the Creator God. In a series of spoken commands, God brings order out of the chaos. In a beautiful poetic sequence, God speaks a good creation into existence. After parting the waters to make night and day, land and sky, and plant and animal life, God concludes with the creation of humanity in God's image. With all creation ordered and crowned with humans as God's image bearers, God declares it all very good. Creation concludes when God celebrates the first Sabbath on the seventh day as a day of rest from the work of creation.

Although in contemporary America the opening chapters of Genesis have gotten caught up in debates about evolution and creationism, this was not so for the earliest Jews and Christians. None of them read the opening chapter of Genesis as a scientific account. What was more important was the truth that the creation story taught about the ordering of the world. Genesis 1 was a kind of origin story, a poem meant to explain the order of the world and humanity's place in it. God created an ordered world but was separate from the creation. There was a split between Creator and creation. As the Apostles' Creed declares, "we believe in God the Father Almighty, maker of heaven and earth."

It is important not only that God is the Creator but that the creation is good. It is the outgrowth of God's goodness, with human beings created in the image of God and set up as caretakers of God's good creation. The whole creation is the work of God's word, which spoke it into existence. The whole cosmos is the work of God's wisdom. As the psalmist declares, "The heavens are telling the glory of God, and the firmament proclaims his handiwork" (Ps 19:1). God's glory is reflected in the good creation. Knowledge of God's wisdom can come from a keen awareness of God's creation.

It is from this framework that we can understand the personification of wisdom in creation in Prov 8. Smack-dab in the middle of Proverbs' recounting of wisdom is a song that is sung by Wisdom personified (scholars often refer to her as *sophia*, the Greek word for wisdom). Building on the idea in Prov 3:19 that "the LORD by wisdom founded the earth," Prov 8 offers a deep dive into Wisdom's role in creation. Wisdom came forth from God before there was any creation, and as God started the process of creation, Wisdom was present. Wisdom was beside God in creation as a master crafts-man that delighted and rejoiced in God, God's world, and humanity (Prov 8:30–31). Proverbs joins wisdom and creation to the one true God. The God of the universe created through Wisdom, and thus the creation reveals the wisdom of the one God. In order for this to make sense, Wisdom had to share in God's presence. Just as we might say that we know an author through their writings or we recognize a friend because of their voice, God creates the world through Wisdom, and by understanding wisdom, one learns of God. Wisdom is not a second god, but rather an expression of the one God's actions in the world.

It is from this perspective that the second verse of "O Come, O Come Emmanuel" knits together creation and wisdom. Wisdom has ordered all of creation as the outworking of God's power and glory. All of the world has been ordered by the one God of Israel, but it has been enacted through God's wisdom. There is an order to the world, and it reveals the wisdom of the one true God. But hidden in this verse is also a mystery. This wisdom of God is not merely reflected in the order of creation. Rather, this wisdom is a person, the Wisdom on high, that has come down from God to guide humanity to knowledge. In order to understand that claim, we have to turn to the opening of John's Gospel, where Wisdom is redefined as the Word made flesh.

JESUS AS WISDOM

The opening of John's Gospel is pretty well known in Christian circles. It offers a kind of bird's-eye view of God's purposes for the world revealed in Jesus as the Word who is with God, who is God, and who became flesh to make God known to the world. But in the hurry to get to the climax of the story, the celebration of Jesus as coming to earth as the Christ child, the beauty and brilliance of the prologue is often lost. Indeed, our familiarity with it often prevents us from seeing the surprise of the opening. After all, Jesus is not actually named until verse 17! In order to understand our hymn's depiction of Wisdom on high, we have to listen closely to the surprising unfolding of John 1.

John's Gospel begins, as it were, at the beginning, with a kind of retelling of Gen 1. The opening words are meant to send the reader back to the start of the biblical story: "in the beginning." But in its dramatic retelling of Gen 1, John's Gospel introduces a new character. For in the beginning, there was not only God but also the Word that is with God and is God. This Word was active in creation, for "all things came into being through him, and without him not one thing came into being" (John 1:3). As a retelling of the creation story, this Word has taken on the characteristics of Wisdom from Prov 8. The Word, like Wisdom, is responsible for God's creation and is an extension of God's creative activity. Like Wisdom, the Word is both distinct from God but also is God.

John further describes this Wisdom as light and life that comes to a people in darkness. We will talk about that light/darkness contrast in another chapter, but even those categories echo the creation account of Genesis, where God creates light and separates it from darkness. But in John 1, this Word comes as the true light that enlightens all people. This Word is meant to lead people back to God (John 1:12). Like the purpose of Wisdom in Proverbs as instructing children to fear the Lord, whoever believes and receives this Word will become a child of God. The whole quest for wisdom explored in ancient cultures and in the Old Testament is now presented as an invitation to receive the Word.

It is clear that John is using the idea of Wisdom's role in creation from the Old Testament but has decided to rename Wisdom "the Word" (in Greek, the *Logos*). But why does he do this? A couple options immediately present themselves. First, Gen 1 tells us that God *spoke* creation into existence. The idea that it was God's speech that ordered creation is an easy way to link the Word with the Wisdom of Prov 8. A similar idea can be found in the writings of many ancient Jewish rabbis. Second, John's Gospel was written in a period where many ancient philosophers often spoke of the Logos as a principal of intelligent order that governed the universe. Just as John says that all can become children of God through believing this Word, so also he is suggesting that all of the attempts of the ancient philosophers to uncover the principle of order in the universe can be found in the Word. Like Proverbs borrowing wisdom sayings from other cultures, John has used a term from Greek philosophy and reworked it in light of his understanding of God in Christ. In both instances, John 1 has tried to communicate that this Word is the source of order and wisdom behind all creation.[2] This paves the way for John's most shocking claim: "And the Word became flesh and lived among us" (John 1:14).

The culmination of the quest for wisdom is found not in humans finally grasping wisdom, but in Wisdom coming down to earth and taking on flesh in the person of Jesus the Messiah. As Paul explains in Col 1:16–17 (also appealing to the figure of Wisdom), Jesus "is the image of the invisible God, the firstborn of all creation, for in him all things in heaven and on earth were created . . . . He

2. For a discussion of the background to John 1, see Smith, *John*, 47–65.

himself is before all things, and in him all things hold together." Wisdom comes down to us as Jesus and reveals God's glory to the world. As "O Come, O Come Emmanuel" declares, "O come, O Wisdom from on high."

BEING GRASPED BY WISDOM

But if wisdom is revealed through creation, why did Wisdom need to come down? Why can't we just look to creation to find our way to God? Behind the declaration of Jesus as Wisdom is a bigger picture that recognizes that something is wrong with creation and our role in it. While uncovering the wisdom behind creation is treated by the Old Testament as a possibility, there nevertheless remains a significant barrier to human attempts to grasp wisdom.

The problem is already established in the book of Genesis. While Gen 1 declares that all of creation is the good work of the good God, the goodness of creation is quickly marred by human disobedience. As Genesis continues, we learn that Adam and Eve, the first humans, were invited to live as God's image bearers in the world and given a commandment from God that they should not eat from the tree of the knowledge of good and evil (Gen 2:16–17). However, through a mixture of deception from the serpent and their own disobedience, Adam and Eve broke the commandment and disobeyed God (Gen 3:1–7). The effects were catastrophic for the entire created order. Pain, suffering, sin, and death were introduced into the world. Sin impacted humanity's relationships with each other, the rest of the world, and their Creator. While much can be said about the disastrous consequences of "the fall" (the term often given to the disobedience of Adam and Eve and its ongoing effects), I simply want to point out that as a story about human attempts to grasp wisdom, it reveals that humans have failed to properly seek God's wisdom in the world. When commanded by God not to take the fruit, Adam and Eve disobeyed. They rejected the wisdom of God expressed in the command and followed their own path, with disastrous results. Disobedience distorts humanity and twists our abilities to see God and seek God's wisdom in the world.

Humanity abandoned God's wisdom and sought to get wisdom on their own. But what they found was only darkness, wickedness, and disobedience.

Our modern quests for wisdom have followed a similar disastrous path that continues to reveal our own wickedness. We have abused God's good creation by polluting our own rivers, leveling our forests, and devastating our climate. We have used science to create atomic bombs and gas chambers. We have invented reasons for treating one another as second-class citizens and as slaves. As one prayer of confession in the UMC hymnal declares, "We have not done your will, we have broken your law, we have rebelled against your love, we have not loved our neighbors, and we have not heard the cry of the needy."[3] In short, we have abandoned God's wisdom.

But in the midst of our darkness, we hear the good news of our Advent hymn. Wisdom has come from on high to show us the path of knowledge and to teach us to go in its way. Although we in the world did not know true wisdom, Wisdom came down to us and revealed God's glory. All are invited to receive and believe in this Wisdom, to come to know Jesus the Messiah, and to be drawn back to God through obedience to Wisdom in the flesh. All of those sages and philosophers seeking wisdom are pointed toward the arrival of Wisdom in the manger. Although we could not find our way to wisdom, Wisdom came down to us to show us the path to God.

CONCLUSION

The second verse of "O Come, O Come Emmanuel" offers us a bird's-eye view of the arrival of Jesus the Messiah. Drawing on the story of creation in Genesis and the role of Wisdom in creation from Proverbs, the Advent hymn captures the universal longing for wisdom as a way to make sense of the world. From the Jewish rabbis to the Greek philosophers, all sought to understand the order of the world and attain the wisdom of the Creator. But humans—both then and now—fail to be wise and obedient. In response, the Advent hymn cries out for Wisdom to come down from on high and show

3. *United Methodist Hymnal*, 8.

humans the path to true knowledge. The Gospel of John expresses that same cry, as it depicts Jesus as the Word that comes down to humanity sitting in darkness to offer light and life. Wisdom comes to us at Christmas. By receiving Wisdom, we are shown our way back to God. Where can wisdom be found? Wisdom is here in the Christ child. Wisdom is present in the church that worships the Word made Flesh. And just as this Wisdom came once, it will come again in glory at the end of days.

DISCUSSION QUESTIONS FOR CHAPTER 2

1. Can you think of a person you consider wise? How is being wise different from being smart?
2. How do you see God's wisdom reflected in creation? Where do you see God's wisdom in the ordering of the world?
3. Do you think that humans have used God's wisdom well or poorly? Can you give examples of each?
4. Have you ever been "grasped by Wisdom"? What was it like to be led into Wisdom's light? How does understanding Jesus as Wisdom help us understand his meaning for our lives and our churches?
5. Read John 1:1–14. What does it say about Jesus before his birth? How does this expand your understanding of the expectations of Advent?

3

Lord of Might

O come, O come, great Lord of might
Who to your tribes on Sinai's height
In ancient times did give the law
In cloud and majesty and awe.

Who is like you, O Lord, *among the gods?*
 Who is like you, majestic in holiness,
 awesome in splendor, doing wonders?
You stretched out your right hand,
 the earth swallowed them.
In your steadfast love you led the people whom you redeemed;
 you guided them by your strength to your holy abode.
The peoples heard, they trembled;
 pangs seized the inhabitants of Philistia.
Then the chiefs of Edom were dismayed;
 trembling seized the leaders of Moab;
 all the inhabitants of Canaan melted away.
Terror and dread fell upon them;
 by the might of your arm, they became still as a stone
until your people, O Lord, *passed by,*
 until the people whom you acquired passed by.

You brought them in and planted them on the mountain of
your own possession,
> *the place, O LORD, that you made your abode,*
> *the sanctuary, O LORD, that your hands have established.*
The LORD will reign forever and ever. (Exod 15:11–18)

In the sixth month the angel Gabriel was sent by God to a
town in Galilee called Nazareth, to a virgin engaged to a man
whose name was Joseph, of the house of David. The virgin's
name was Mary. And he came to her and said, "Greetings,
favored one! The Lord is with you." But she was much per-
plexed by his words and pondered what sort of greeting this
might be. The angel said to her, "Do not be afraid, Mary, for
you have found favor with God. And now, you will conceive
in your womb and bear a son, and you will name him Jesus.
He will be great, and will be called the Son of the Most High,
and the Lord God will give to him the throne of his ancestor
David. He will reign over the house of Jacob forever, and of his
kingdom there will be no end." Mary said to the angel, "How
can this be, since I am a virgin?" The angel said to her, "The
Holy Spirit will come upon you, and the power of the Most
High will overshadow you; therefore the child to be born will
be holy; he will be called Son of God. And now, your relative
Elizabeth in her old age has also conceived a son; and this is
the sixth month for her who was said to be barren. For nothing
will be impossible with God." Then Mary said, "Here am I, the
servant of the Lord; let it be with me according to your word."
Then the angel departed from her. (Luke 1:26–38)

FROM WISDOM TO LAW

During graduate school, I spent a lot of time traveling to and from
Atlanta. While I am sure many large cities can claim to have horrible

traffic, in my experience, Atlanta traffic is the absolute worst. I spent hours stuck in bumper-to-bumper traffic on interstates with five or more lanes. It was not uncommon for my two-hour commute to run four hours or more. However, there was always at least one lane that was less crowded called the HOV lane. Set aside for "high-occupancy vehicles" (hence the acronym HOV), this was a lane designated for cars with multiple people in them. This special lane always seemed to move quicker than the other lanes. Recently, Atlanta has also added another special lane for cars willing to buy a special pass. Both lanes are meant to provide a solution to the traffic issue by creating spaces to keep drivers moving, even if they are only extended to certain people. Of course, these special lanes are only as good as their ability to cut down traffic time and became subject, over time, to the same traffic issues as the rest of the lanes. They became overused and had car accidents that slowed them down, just like the other lanes. But, at least at the outset, they were a way some people could avoid the nightmare of Atlanta traffic.

In our third verse of "O Come, O Come Emmanuel," we are taken from a focus on the universal appeal of wisdom to God's special gift of the law to Israel. While wisdom was extended to all people and was revealed through God's creation, the revelation of God through the Mosaic law was extended to a particular group, God's chosen people, the Israelites. While both wisdom and law lead to God, they are also distinct. They are somewhat analogous to the different lanes of the Atlanta interstate. Wisdom was crowded and beset with issues that arose from the effects of original sin. The law, however, was like Israel's HOV lane, giving them special access to God. To understand the role of the law and its significance for Jesus' arrival means returning again to the Old Testament.

Following Israel's deliverance from slavery in Egypt through the exodus, God called the Israelites to Mount Sinai. As they assembled around the mountain, God appeared to them in a terrifying, dark cloud Israel was afraid to approach the mountain and instead sent Moses up as their representative. Moses was then given the gift of the law as a kind of constitution for the people of Israel. The law was meant to set Israel apart as God's people. While wisdom is universal, God's law was Israel's special guidance from God. Exodus explains the contrast between wisdom and the law: "Indeed, the whole earth is mine, but you shall be for me a priestly kingdom and a holy nation" (Exod 19:5b–6a). While God created all things through wisdom, the law was given to set Israel apart from the rest of the world as a holy people. Israel's unique status, often called election, would be the means by which God could rescue the rest of the world. Alongside the gift of the law was the promise of God's ongoing presence with Israel, first in the tabernacle and subsequently in the temple. Israel would be a holy people, not least because the holy God would dwell in their midst. Law and presence revealed Israel's special vocation in the world.

While the law seemed like a solution, a special lane for certain people offering them a more straightforward path of obedience and commitment to the one God, this plan eventually proved ineffective. As we will see, the law eventually revealed Israel's shortcomings and contributed to the departure of God's tabernacling presence. But the promise of the law and the image of the tabernacle also point to the arrival of Israel's Messiah. For this Messiah, as Paul explains, was born of a woman and born under the law (Gal 4:4).

MOUNT SINAI: LAW AND TABERNACLE

The third verse of "O Come, O Come Emmanuel" celebrates the Lord of might, who appeared to the tribes of Israel at Sinai's height with the gift of the law. The image takes us to the middle of the book of Exodus to the people gathered around a mountain in the Sinai Desert. The story of the exodus is *the foundational event* for the people of Israel in the Old Testament. It is the moment when God delivered the people from slavery in Egypt, a great act of salvation that forever shaped Israel's understanding of themselves and their relationship with the God of their ancestors. The exodus is to the Old Testament what the crucifixion of Jesus is to the New Testament. It is the mighty act of God's salvation.

But the third verse of our Advent hymn does not take us to the exodus itself. Rather, we are invited to envision what comes after the deliverance from Egypt. Israel, previously enslaved under an oppressive Pharaoh, had seen God act in powerful and destructive ways for their deliverance. They saw God part the Red Sea so they could flee the pursuit of Pharaoh's army. When they had crossed safely, God brought the waters crashing down on the army in a singular act of destruction. Israel was finally free. Exod 15 presents the song that Moses and the Israelites sang in response. It celebrates God's power, strength, and deliverance of Israel through the waters of the sea. It praises the God who is "majestic in holiness, awesome in splendor" (Exod 15:12). It declares that there is no other God like Israel's God (Exod 15:11). It notes Israel's unique place in God's creation. For God chose the people of Israel for redemption through God's steadfast love, and God put fear into all of the hearts of those who opposed Israel. It is a song that celebrates election.

But the song also closes by acknowledging where Israel is heading: "You brought them in and planted them on the mountain of your own possession, the place, O LORD, that you made your abode, the sanctuary, O LORD, that your hands have established" (Exod 15:17). Mount Sinai is set apart as a special place of God's dwelling, a sign of God's presence.[1] Although God rules the whole world and created all things, this place of God's dwelling was set apart. The arrival at this mountain actually frames the entire exodus narrative. For it was on this same mountain that God appeared to Moses in the burning bush, revealed God's name as YHWH (in translation, it is usually written LORD), and sent Moses to deliver the Israelites from slavery (Exod 3:1–11). God also declared that the sign of God's presence with Moses would be that the people would worship God on this holy mountain after they left Egypt. The arrival to the mountain after the exodus was a fulfilled promise.

But if the arrival at the mountain marked the end of the exodus, it also signaled a new beginning for the people of Israel. When God appeared to Israel on the mountain, God also gave the people

1. There is an overlap of terms for this mountain in the literature. In Exod 3:1, it is called Horeb. A similar name is used elsewhere for the mountain where Moses is given the law, as in Deut 4:10, 15; 5:2; 1 Kgs 8:9. It is also where Israel makes the golden calf, as in Ps 106:19. The same place is described as Mount Sinai in Exod 19. Our Advent hymn "O Come, O Come Emmanuel" assumes they are the same place, as suggested by some scholars. See Meyers, *Exodus*, 152.

the law and the description of the tabernacle. The law was a kind of constitution for ordering the life of the people as a community in relationship with God and one another. The tabernacle was a kind of tent that would serve as sanctuary for God's presence with the people of Israel on their journey. The law and the tabernacle become two foundational items that shaped the identity of the people of Israel. They were what set them apart as God's chosen people, a priestly nation for the world. Let us take these two items in their turn.

First, God gave Israel the gift of the law at Sinai, captured initially in the Ten Commandments (Exod 20) and followed by a series of rules and regulations for the life of the Israelite community. For Israel, the law was not a punishment from God but a constitution to help the Israelites live into their unique vocation as God's people. If God was the King of Israel (Exod 15:18), God had the authority to decide the rules that ought to govern the life of the Israelites. These rules covered all aspects of life, from the religious practices of the community (e.g., sacrifices, priesthood, and festivals) to the relationships between community members (e.g., laws about property, slaves, and restitution for wrongdoing). But standing over them all was a deep obedience to God alone, who had delivered Israel from slavery (Exod 20:1). To keep the law was to obey the voice of God. But keeping the law did not *earn* God's salvation. God had already saved Israel in the exodus! Rather, keeping the law was an act of thankfulness to and love for the God who had rescued Israel. Throughout Israel's history, law keeping became a significant way to love the Lord (cf. Deut 6:1–9).

Second, God gave Israel the gift of God's presence. God promised to be with the people through the tabernacle they would create. Of course, God had been with Israel throughout the exodus, just as God was with them now on the mountain. But God's presence was overwhelming and terrifying. Indeed, God's presence in the dark cloud, smoke, thunder, and lighting was so terrifying that only Moses ascended the mountain. God's voice was so awe-inspiring that the people insisted on staying at a distance. They preferred to hear Moses' report from God rather than God's voice. God's presence, as the hymn declares, reveals the Lord of might with majesty and awe.

As part of the law, therefore, God introduced mediation between the people and God. Israel would not encounter the presence of God face to face. Rather, God would be with Israel in the tabernacle. The tabernacle was a tent-like structure that Israel would set up in their camp as the place where God would dwell among them (Exod 25:8). When the tabernacle was finally built, the cloud of God's presence covered the tent, and "the glory of the Lord filled the tabernacle" (Exod 40:34). Not only did God give Israel the law, God dwelled with the people in the tabernacle. Eventually in Israel's history, the tabernacle was replaced by the temple built by Solomon (2 Kgs 5–8). Just as God had dwelt in the tabernacle, so God dwelt with Israel in the temple in Jerusalem. When the temple was dedicated, the same cloud of God's glory filled the temple as it had done in the tabernacle.

Hence the declaration in our hymn that the gift of Sinai is "the law in cloud and majesty and awe." The gift of the law came alongside the presence of God with the people in the tabernacle, a presence that was majestic and awe-inspiring. Both elements worked to set Israel apart as the unique people of God called to be holy in the world. If the law served as Israel's constitution to order their lives toward one another and God, the tabernacle served as a continual reminder of God's presence with the people. Both reinforced their identity around the God they worshiped in thankfulness. But as the story of Israel continued, the law and the tabernacle revealed a deep brokenness in Israel's obedience to God that would invite the return of the Lord in the Christ child.

A BROKEN LAW AND A DEPARTING CLOUD

Although God's gifts of the law and the tabernacle were a blessing that set Israel apart from the nations, it quickly becomes apparent in Exodus that there were deep flaws with this arrangement. Israel was chosen to be a holy nation and a royal priesthood, but they were prone to the same disobedience and sinfulness as the rest of the world. Even though they were chosen by God, they still fell short of living into God's holy calling. And so, as the story of God and Israel unfolds in the Old Testament, we see the gift of the law scorned through disobedience. Accompanying this disobedience, we also see the retreat of God's presence from Israel as the cloud of glory departed. To draw on our earlier analogy, it was as if there was now traffic clogging up the HOV lane.

The flaws in Israel's vocation to be God's obedient people were already apparent at the foot of Mount Sinai. While Israel was waiting for Moses to come down from the mountain with the law, they grew anxious and decided to create an image of their own god out of gold (Exod 32:1). With the image erected, they held a festival honoring this idol at the base of Mount Sinai, and the high priest declared, "These are your gods, O Israel, who brough you up out of the land of Egypt!" (Exod 32:4). This event seems almost unthinkable for us today. How could Israel abandon the worship of the Lord who had delivered them from slavery in Egypt? How could they forget the God who was on the mountain in the cloud with awe and majesty? How could Israel break the law so quickly and forget their God?

Before we accuse Israel of such flagrant disobedience and forgetfulness, we might turn those challenges back on ourselves. How often do we forget the worship of the one true God to serve things that are not of God? How often do we run off after the gods of power, sex, and money and forget the blessings of God in our life? As I once heard a fellow Christian tell a gathering of Christian leaders who were discussing our current immigration policies in America, "I love the Lord and follow Jesus, but we should not receive the immigrants. At this point, it seems best for us just to forget the teaching of Jesus." Regardless of your political stance, if you find yourself simultaneously claiming to love God but willfully abandoning God's commands, you are on the doorstep of idolatry and disobedience. For at the center of both Israel's disobedience and our disobedience lies a common flaw. The distorting effects of sin have warped us, just as sin warped the Israelites. Just as we are broken and sit in darkness, so also Israel continually rejected obedience and sinned in the Old Testament. God's good gift of the law only ended up imprisoning Israel until the truly faithful one arrived (cf. Gal 3:23–25).

The incident with the golden calf reveals the cracks in Israel's identity as God's people that continued to spread throughout the Old Testament. This moment of idolatry is not isolated. Israel would continue to worship other gods, even after they entered the promised land. They would reject God as their king, opting instead for human kings that often lead them further into disobedience. As Israel abandoned the worship of their God, they would also forget other aspects of the law. They would forget to follow God's call of justice and righteousness for the poor and vulnerable among them. They would distort justice, exploit the poor, and oppress the weak. As a result, judgment would come upon them. As noted in our discussion of the first verse of "O Come, O Come Emmanuel," the exile was described as God's judgment on Israel's disobedience. And Israel still felt stuck in exile at the time of the birth of Jesus.

But what of the presence of God? What happened to God's presence with Israel in the tabernacle and then in the temple? The prophet Ezekiel offers a devasting picture of the departure of God's glory from the temple. He received a vision of the abominations taking place in the temple, abominations including the worship of idols, that God declared would "drive me far from my sanctuary" (Ezek 8:6). Ezekiel then depicts the glory of the Lord, the cloud of majesty and awe, rising up from the temple and departing (Ezek 11). Ezekiel had these visions in the wake of the exile. It seems that the departure of God's glory from the temple conveyed the sense that God's presence departed from the temple before its terrible destruction by the Babylonians. The exile coincided with the departure of God's presence. The cloud departed from Israel in response to their disobedience.

But this is not the whole story. For the prophecies of Ezekiel close with a vision of the return of God's glory to a new temple. In a vision that recalls the appearance of God at Mount Sinai (Exod 19), the dwelling of God in the tabernacle (Exod 40:34), and the glory entering the temple of Solomon (2 Kgs 5–8), Ezekiel sees the glory of God return to a rebuilt temple. Ezekiel is overwhelmed by the reversal of God's departing presence when God's glory enters this new, cleansed, and perfected temple (Ezek 43:1–12). Ezekiel's vision inspired Israel's hope in exile that God would return to dwell with God's people. Israel longed for God to be Emmanuel, God with them, just as God had once dwelt among them in ancient times. This longing remained after the end of the exile, even when the temple was rebuilt. For God did not return in glory as anticipated. The rebuilt temple is never depicted as having the same glory, that cloud of majesty and awe, that characterized the initial presence of God or the prophetic vision of Ezekiel (cf. Ezra 3:12–13). Israel was still waiting.

MARY AND THE NEW TABERNACLE

Among those who were waiting for God's returning glory was a young woman in the small village of Nazareth named Mary. Mary was engaged to Joseph when she received a miraculous visit from the angel Gabriel. As Luke 1:26–28 recounts the story, the angel declares to Mary that she has found favor with God and will give birth to a child. But this will be no ordinary child. The child will be named Jesus, and he will be the Son of the Most High. God will give him the throne of David and he will reign over Israel forever. Mary is the recipient of the fulfillment of God's promises for a coming Messiah, the one who will be faithful in all of the ways Israel has fallen short and who will fulfill Israel's vocation. God's great story for Israel was finally approaching its fulfillment.

But Mary reacts to this visit with a question: "How can this be, since I am a virgin?" (Luke 1:34). It is at this point that the background of the tabernacle becomes so important. The angel explains to Mary that her child will be a miracle, for "the Holy Spirit will come upon you, and the power of the Most High will overshadow you" (Luke 1:35). This child is no ordinary child but will be God made flesh. In what seems to us a rather strange description of the coming of God in the flesh, the angel explains that Mary will be *overshadowed* by the power of the Most High. The word "overshadowed" (in Greek, *episkiazein*) is the term used to describe God's tabernacling presence. When God's presence fills the tabernacle in Exodus 40:35, the cloud *overshadows* the tent. Luke's Gospel is asking us to see the connection between the two events. Just as God once dwelt with Israel in the tabernacle, so now God's glory has come to reside in Mary's womb. The child born to her will be the presence of God with humanity. John says something similar when he says that the Word became flesh and *dwelt* among us. The word used for "dwelt" is related to the word for "tabernacle" in Greek. Thus, one could translate John 1:14 as "The Word became flesh and *tabernacled* among us." In both passages, the image of the birth of Christ is seen as the return of God's presence with the people in a way analogous to the presence of God in the tabernacle or in the temple in glory. This itself is a reiteration of the promise explored in our first chapter when Jesus is given the name Emmanuel. The long-awaited return of God has arrived in Jesus. The divine presence has chosen a new temple, the womb of this woman in Nazareth.

Mary herself realizes the significance of this good news. In the song she sings in the presence of Elizabeth a few verses later, Mary rejoices in God her savior and sets a tone of joy for God's arrival. She celebrates God as the Mighty One (Luke 1:49), recalling the declaration that the power of the Most High will overshadow her (Luke 1:35). She also understands this coming child as the fulfillment of God's hope for Israel—the hope that they will show God's love to the world, which they had failed to do in their disobedience. Though the coming child, God "has helped his servant Israel, in remembrance of his mercy, according to the promise he made to our ancestors, to Abraham and to his descendants forever" (Luke 1:54–55 NRSV). As the Advent hymn prays for the return of the Lord of might, so Mary announces to the world that the Mighty One has returned. God's presence is dwelling with the people again. This presence is now encountered in the child born to her. This presence will mean Israel's deliverance, as well as the salvation of the whole world. Where Israel has fallen short of God's plan, the Christ child will bring it through to completion.

CONCLUSION

The third verse of "O Come, O Come Emmanuel" takes us to the momentous events of the exodus that culminate in God's appearance at

Mount Sinai, the gift of the law, and the promise of God's presence in the tabernacle. The gifts of God's law and presence are meant to be a source of great joy for the people. They are meant to encourage Israel's obedience. Yet what they expose is Israel's failure to live into their election. The law is broken. The dwelling presence of God departs. But that is not the end of the story. For, in the words of the angel to Mary and in her beautiful song, we learn that Israel has not been forgotten. A child will be born who will be the new dwelling presence of God, who will keep the law faithfully where others have failed. The Lord of might will descend again, this time as a helpless babe, in order to deliver the whole world.

DISCUSSION QUESTIONS FOR CHAPTER 3

1. How does this chapter use the metaphor of traffic to explain the relationship between wisdom and law?
2. What is the purpose of the law in the Old Testament? How often have you heard the law spoken of in church? How does this relate to what is presented here?
3. This chapter describes the law and God's presence as two marks of Israel's identity. What was their role? How did they show the world Israel's role as God's chosen people?
4. How do you struggle with idolatry despite knowing God? How is your plight like that of Israel at the foot of Mount Sinai?
5. How does the language of the tabernacle help us understand the birth of Jesus?

4

The Branch and the Tree

O come, O Branch of Jesse's stem
Unto your own and rescue them!
From depths of hell your people save,
And give them victory o'er the grave.

A shoot shall come out from the stump of Jesse,
*   and a branch shall grow out of his roots.*
The spirit of the LORD *shall rest on him,*
*   the spirit of wisdom and understanding,*
*   the spirit of counsel and might,*
*   the spirit of knowledge and the fear of the* LORD.
His delight shall be in the fear of the LORD.
He shall not judge by what his eyes see,
*   or decide by what his ears hear. (Isa 11:1–3)*

Blessed be the Lord God of Israel,
*   for he has looked favorably on his people and redeemed*
*   them.*
He has raised up a mighty savior for us
*   in the house of his servant David,*
as he spoke through the mouth of his holy prophets from of old

that we would be saved from our enemies and from the
hand of all who hate us. (Luke 1:68–71)

PLANTING FOR THE FUTURE

When I was in elementary school, we regularly had special events on Earth Day. One year we even took a trip to the Illinois State Fair Grounds to join in the celebration with other students. We saw science experiments about photosynthesis and learned about the importance of recycling. We also got a bag full of free swag to remember the event. The most interesting gift was a little green plant in a black plastic pot. As one of the presenters explained to us, this was the start of a tree. It was a seed that was just beginning to break through the dirt. We were invited to take this little shoot home and bury it in our yard. As we watered and cared for it, one day it would become a big tree. There was just one problem with this plan. The people at Earth Day did not tell us what type of tree it would become. Turns out, it was the shoot of a cottonwood tree, likely chosen because they grow quickly and are rather hardy. However, there was a downside to the cottonwood tree. As my parents explained, we would not be planting it in our yard because every spring, cottonwoods produce a cotton-like seed that covers the yard like snow. While that might seem pretty, these seedlings get everywhere and are a complete pain in the neck to clean up. The last thing my parents wanted in their yard was a cottonwood tree that made a huge mess.

Of course, how was I supposed to know what a cottonwood tree would look like based on this little twig in a pot? After all, it takes quite a bit of imagination to go from the tiny shoot to a massive tree. Just think about it for a moment. How strange is it that something as small as an acorn, a little tiny nut, could become a large oak tree? Or that the prickly pinecone contains pine nuts that will eventually become a pine tree? The seed and the tree are often worlds apart.

In the fourth verse of "O Come, O Come Emmanuel," we are introduced to the image of the branch of Jesse's tree. The branch (or shoot or root, as it is sometimes translated) is a metaphor derived from gardening. It is a small part of a tree that, when planted, can grow into a full-sized tree. This image was one way of talking about Israel's coming Messiah in the Bible. But wrapped up in the image is also something of an enigma. For the similarities between a tiny branch and the full-grown tree are often hard to detect. It takes a careful eye and willing imagination to see the possibility of a tree in a mere shoot. The same is true for the Messiah. As we will see, the shoot was derived from the imagery of the tree of Jesse, the promise given to King David and his descendants. But the messianic shoot, like a tiny seedling, could grow in unexpected and surprising ways that looked quite different from what many expected.

FROM THE MOUNTAIN TO THE TREE

To understand the messianic tree imagery, we actually need to go back to the event at Mount Sinai. At the center of the gift of the law and the promise of God's presence is the insistence that the LORD is the God and King of Israel. As the great Exodus hymn exclaims, "The LORD will reign forever and ever" (Exod 15:18). Israel's king is to be God, and the people are to be God's priestly kingdom and holy nation. Although God created the whole universe, God chooses Israel to be a special people and desires to reign over them as their King.

But Israel struggles with this political arrangement. Once they enter into the promised land, they begin to realize that all of the other nations have kings to rule over them and lead them in battle. Israel does not have a human king, so Israel begins to beg God to give them a king to rule over them. God eventually gives in to their request, but it is hardly a step forward for Israel. God explains that in asking for a king, "they have rejected me from being king over them" (1 Sam 8:7). God draws a parallel with their breaking of the law and their worship of other gods, explaining that the rejection of God's kingship is an outgrowth of the same disobedience in Israel's heart that has led them to idolatry. Like a sickness that causes a runny nose, a terrible cough, and bodily soreness, so Israel's sinfulness affects their law-keeping, their worship of God, and their political rule. These are all symptoms of the same sickness of sin.

When God gives Israel a king, God also warns Israel of the danger of a king. Because kings have such power and authority, they can do great good or harm for the people. The harm they can bring includes exploitative taxation, constant warfare, increased slavery, and living in luxury off the labor of their own subjects (1 Sam 8:10–18). The king's power and influence often deceives him into thinking he is above the law and will not be judged. As a result, kings are prone to deadly pride and often try to take the place of the one God of Israel. The history of the kings of Israel (and Judah) reveals just how dangerous kings can be, with the worst of them creating a toxic culture that promotes the worship of other gods and practices of oppression and injustice. A quick scan of 1–2 Kings, the story of the kings of Israel and Judah, reveals an overwhelming number of terrible and unfaithful rulers. And where the ruler leads, the nation follows. The unfaithful leadership of Israel and Judah eventually lead the people into unfaithfulness. The end result of these kings is the exile, God's judgment on Israel as a whole for their unfaithfulness.

But not all of the kings of Israel are unfaithful. Rather, kingship is a mixed blessing, as God is able to work some good out of Israel's request for a king. While Saul, the first king of Israel, shows himself to be rather disobedient, the second king of Israel becomes the ideal for all the kings of Israel. The second king's name is David. He is anointed as a young man, the youngest of the children of Jesse, from the town of Bethlehem (1 Sam 16). David proves himself to be a brilliant military leader by his defeat of Goliath and his leadership in Saul's army. After Saul's death, he takes control over the nation of Israel and leads the people into a glorious golden age with military success and abounding prosperity. Of course, King David is not himself perfect, as his sexual assault of Bathsheba and subsequent murder of her husband reveals (2 Sam 11–12). Yet, David continually strives to be faithful to the God of Israel and to promote that faithfulness in the nation. This earns him the description of a man after God's own heart (1 Sam 13:14).

O COME EMMANUEL

One of the ways that David shows himself faithful to the God of Israel is by asking to build a temple for the worship of the one God in Jerusalem. God responds to this request by reminding David that never once has God asked to be housed in a temple, but rather has resided in the tabernacle in order to journey with the people (2 Sam 7:5–7). But in a remarkable shift, God agrees to let one of David's descendants build a temple for him in Jerusalem. God also takes the request and amplifies it by making a promise with David. As David has sought to build a house for the Lord, God will also build a house out of David. God will ensure that a king from David's lineage will reign over Israel forever. As God explains, "Your house and your kingdom shall be made sure forever before me; your throne shall be established forever" (2 Sam 7:16). Wrapped up in this is a promise expressed through the language of sonship: the king will be as a son to God. As 2 Samuel 7:14a explains, "I will be a father to him, and he shall be a son to me."

Through this promise, David becomes the ideal for kingship in Israelite history. The covenant with David and his family also becomes a significant factor in all of the messianic hopes in later biblical history. At this point, it might be helpful to describe briefly what "messiah" actually means. It comes from a Hebrew word for anointing (*mashach*), a ritual practice of pouring oil on someone in order to consecrate or set them apart for a special task or duty. In Greek, the equivalent of anointing language is christening (in Greek, *chrio*). The terms "messiah" and "christ" are the Hebrew and Greek terms that both refer to an anointed person. Various people were anointed in the Bible for specific tasks, such as priests or kings. For instance, both David and Saul were anointed as kings. But because David was an anointed king, the language of an anointed one was often joined to the promise of a future king in the line of David. Thus, messianic language was often connected to hopes of a future Davidic king of Israel. To throw another metaphor on top of this, anointing was also combined with sonship. Just as King David was called God's son, so the future messianic hopes were often attached to language of kingly sonship. Messiah, anointing, sonship, and Davidic lineage are all connected in the Bible. This provides the soil from which hopes for a future Messiah sprouted.

During the reign of King David and his son Solomon, Israel flourishes. The temple of God is built in Jerusalem, and the nation experiences a great sense of peace and prosperity. The tree of the Davidic kingship blossoms and is in full bloom. God blesses the people through their faithful king as the people joined together in the worship of the one true God in Jerusalem. In the Old Testament, this is a golden age for the Israelites. But it is short-lived, for the seasons quickly change from summer to fall. The Davidic tree experiences the approaching autumn, with its leaving falling off in the changing weather. The leaves are already changing under the reign of King Solomon, who, in his old age, begins to turn away from the worship of God to the worship of the other gods of his many wives (1 Kgs 11). God punishes Solomon's disobedience by splitting the kingdom of Israel into the Northern Kingdom of Israel and the Southern Kingdom of Judah. Neither resists the work of evil in their midst, and the end result is the exile spoken of in previous chapters. As 2 Kings puts the matter, "Jerusalem and Judah so angered the LORD that he expelled them from his presence (2 Kgs 24:20). With the invasion of Jerusalem by Babylon, the temple is destroyed and the Davidic tree is stripped bare.

THE DAVIDIC BRANCH

It is during this metaphorical winter of Israel's history that the overlap of anointing, sonship, and the Davidic promise all begin to join together to produce the first signs of new life. The metaphor of the Davidic tree is used by the prophet Isaiah and helps us understand the dominant image in the fourth verse of "O Come, O Come Emmanuel." As Isa 11:1 explains, "A shoot shall come up from the stump of Jesse, and a branch shall grow out of his roots." In the wake of the devastation of the Davidic kingship and the Israelites, Isaiah promises a day where the stump of Jesse will show new life. Jesse was the father of King David. So Isaiah is prophesying that the Davidic promise that an heir will reign on the throne forever is still true. God has not forgotten that promise but will produce new life from this stump. God will raise up a new branch out of the devastation of David's house. There will be a new king to reign on David's throne. Hence the image in the fourth verse of "O Come, O Come Emmanuel": "O come thou Root of Jesse's tree."

But there is more to this promise than just the arrival of a king from the line of David. As the oracle of Isa 11 continues, this coming king will be filled with the fullness of God's spirit and be guided by the fear of the Lord. Like David, he will be a faithful king. He will exhibit the justice and righteousness required by the law. He will not promote oppression but will defeat wickedness. This coming king will not follow the paths of the wicked kings of old. He will be faithful to the law in a way that even David himself had fallen short. As the oracle continues, this king will bring in a period of great peace where even the wolves and lambs will lie down together. In a final, powerful flourish, the prophet declares that pain and destruction will be removed from the holy mountain and "the earth will be full of the knowledge of the LORD as the waters cover the sea" (Isa 11:9). The root of Jesse will become a tree to which all of the nations are invited to come and see the dwelling of God's glory (Isa 11:10). This restored Davidic king will be a blessing for all of the nations and the whole creation. God's plan to fix what was broken in the world, broken in humans, and even broken in Israel is reversed by the king who is faithful to the law, brings peace and justice to the nations, and restores the whole world.

The image of this coming king from David's line is provocative and powerful. It helps Israel forge connections between the promise to David, the hopes of Israel, and the future of the whole world that continues to shape the Old Testament story. A number of the psalms seem to make similar connections as Isa 11. Psalm 2 warns the nations to serve the Lord, for a day is coming when the Lord's anointed ruler, God's chosen son, will bring justice and judgment to the nations. Psalm 89 celebrates God's covenant with David established forever and, in the same breath, calls for God to remember this covenant and restore the Davidic line.

It is not just the psalms that are shaped by this hope for the restoration of the Davidic branch. After Israel returns from exile under the decree of King Cyrus, there are significant attempts to reestablish Israel's glory days. A new temple is built, and there are some latent hopes that this might be the return of God to the people. Alongside this hope, there is also some hope that a new king might emerge over Israel. The prophet Zechariah, for instance, has a vision of two olive trees, which he takes as a sign of the coming of two anointed ones (Zech 4:14). The olive tree has obvious connections to the Davidic tree because of the tree language. But messiahship is also connected to the olive tree because olive oil was often used in anointing. Zechariah uses this language to describe the coming partnership of the high priest Joshua, son of Jehozadak, and the kingly figure Zerubbabel in their restoration of Jerusalem after the exile. Furthermore, Zechariah uses the language of the branch to describe their roles in Israel's hope for future glory (Zech 3:8; 6:11-13). The branch metaphor was already charged as a powerful way of communicating the overlap of so many of Israel's hopes for their future and for God's coming deliverance.

But Zechariah's focus on King Zerubbabel and the high priest Joshua comes and goes without the arrival of a glorious kingdom. The second temple is finished, but God's glory still seems absent. The return of the Davidic king to establish peace and justice never materializes in the Old Testament. Rather, Israel remains subject to one empire or another. The exile in Babylon shifts to Israel's subjugation as a client state to the Persians. The Persians are defeated by the Greeks, and Israel becomes a servant of various Greek kings. While for a moment the nation of Israel wins its independence under the Maccabees, this independence is short-lived and fails to result in a glorious restoration. Rather, the infighting between the leaders of Israel results in Israel's subjugation to the Roman empire. Seasons come and seasons go, but the Davidic tree remains bare. No stem is bursting forth from the stump. The promises remain buried, germinating below the surface in the hearts and minds of the people of God, who long for the first signs of spring and for the first green shoots to burst through the hardened ground.

JESUS, THE ROOT OF JESSE'S STEM

But for those with eyes to see, the birth narratives in the Gospels of Matthew and Luke are adorned with the first leaves of the blossoming branch of Jesse. There is a repeated emphasis that the child born to Mary is from the Davidic line and will be the promised anointed deliverer who will reign on the throne of David. The density of Davidic language is so clear that once one understands the messianic hopes, it stands out in stark relief. In Luke, the virgin Mary is engaged to "Joseph, *of the house of David*" (Luke 1:27, italics added). The angel declares that the child born to her will "be called the *Son of the Most High*," that "the Lord God will give him the *throne of his ancestor David*," and that "he will reign over Israel forever; *his Kingdom will never end!*" (Luke 1:34 NLT, italics added). All of this language invokes the Davidic covenant and the prophetic application of that covenant to the coming messianic figure. A similar collection of Davidic imagery can be found in the opening of Matthew's Gospel. Jesus is "the Messiah, the son of David" (Matt 1:1; cf. 1:18, 20). Indeed, throughout the New Testament, Jesus is understood as the promised Messiah, the Christ. Christ is not Jesus' last name but his title as the anointed ruler from the line of David. It declares his kingship to the world. This is the new branch of the Davidic promise. Revelation makes this image explicit when it declares Jesus to be "the root of David" (Rev 5:5).

But what will the Messiah do? Following the imagery of Isa 11, the promised Messiah will deliver Israel from their enemies and establish justice, righteousness, and peace in the world. This kingly figure will bring deliverance and the defeat of Israel's enemies. This was the initial hope for Jesus the Messiah as well. In anticipation of the birth of Jesus the Messiah, the Gospel of Luke describes the prophetic words of Zechariah, the father of John the Baptist. Zechariah looks forward to the day of the Messiah's arrival, explaining that God "has raised up a mighty savior for us in the house of his servant David" (Luke 1:69). Again, the language of messianic hope is tied to the arrival of the king in David's line. But note that this king is seen as a savior of Israel. As Zechariah continues, this salvation is given a concrete expression. The prophets promised that by the hands of the Messiah "we would be saved from our enemies and from the hand of all who hate us" (Luke 1:71). The Messiah ought to bring deliverance through the defeat of Israel's enemies. Just as David brought peace to Israel by defeating Israel's enemies, so the Davidic Messiah ought to establish the peaceable kingdom through the defeat of Israel's current enemies. But remember, the seed often looks quite different from the tree that it becomes.

This is where there is a curious departure in the Gospels from the messianic hopes of Israel. For the arrival of Jesus does not come with the conquest of Israel's enemies. Roman rule is not overturned by the conquering strength of Jesus the Christ. So, how can Jesus be the Messiah and not conquer Israel's enemies? The Advent hymn "O Come, O Come Emmanuel" provides a helpful Christian redescription of the Messiah's conquest. For Jesus the Messiah comes not to conquer Israel's enemies but to defeat all of the forces of sin and evil in the world. He comes to conquer death. As the hymn declares, "From depths of hell your people save, / And give them victory o'er the grave." Jesus' ultimate enemies are not physical opponents of flesh and blood but the spiritual forces of sin, evil, and death. These forces, introduced to God's good creation by human disobedience, are the opponents of God's Messiah and must be defeated for God's kingdom of peace to come. Throughout Jesus' ministry, the enemy is not defined as specific people that God has come to defeat. Rather, Jesus comes to defeat the enemies that lie inside each of us and pervade the whole world with their corrupting influence.

How are we to explain this shift in Israel's hopes from the Messiah's defeat of Israel's enemies to the defeat of the forces of sin and death? The answer is already revealed to us in Israel's own history. After all, the gift of the king was a mixed blessing. While a king could lead Israel to faithfulness, more often Israel's kings promoted injustice and wickedness in the world, leading the nation astray to the worship of other gods. As much as Israel needed a king to lead the nation in battle against her enemies, Israel's king fell short of transforming the hearts and minds of the people to be the light of God to the world. Rather, the people remained entangled in the chains of sin and death. The arrival of the promised king would have to win a deeper battle than just the defeat of Israel's enemies.

The Messiah would need to win the battle against sin and death going on under the surface of all empires and in every human heart. The earliest Christians declared that Jesus was the Messiah, but his victory was not a physical conquest. Rather, his death and resurrection rescued people from sin and death. As Paul's second letter to Timothy declares, Jesus Christ "abolished death and brought life and immortality to light through the gospel" (2 Tim 1:10). The Messiah born in a manger would indeed defeat Israel's enemies, but it would be the real enemies of sin, evil, and death in the world.

Perhaps an analogy will help us understand this better. In my high school American history class, I remember spending an entire week learning about the civil rights movement. We watched a documentary about the movement that focused on the nonviolent protests of Martin Luther King Jr. and the witness of countless other people of color. I learned the devastating story of Emmet Till and of the courage of Rosa Parks. As I saw the struggle for equality being played out in this film, I finally realized the depth of human sinfulness. For centuries, many Americans had convinced themselves that it was okay to abuse, mistreat, and even kill people based solely on the color of their skin. This evil was embodied not only in institutions and systems of oppression, but in the hearts of the very people I saw in the film abusing a little girl as she entered a school, aiming fire hoses at protesters, and dressed in white robes in order to lynch a black man. Then I thought about the racist jokes and inappropriate racial slurs I had overheard from the adults around me. I saw how these two things were deeply connected. How seemingly good people and those terribly bad people are both marred by the same deep-rooted sinfulness. They share in the wickedness of the world. Racism is just one example, but it would take little to multiply the same patterns of sinfulness around us. How the greed of corporations is often reflected in our own materialism. How the lies of politicians reflect our own failures to speak truth, to be honest with ourselves, to remove our own masks and show our true selves. The real enemies are not simply someone else. Evil runs through every human heart and penetrates the whole of humanity.

Evil runs deep. It is not simply outside us in our enemies—it runs through our very hearts as well. Deliverance, true salvation, will only come when hearts are transformed, along with the wider culture. The peaceable kingdom of the Messiah, the kingdom of justice and righteousness, requires victory at all levels. What that branch of Jesse would proclaim is that the entire tree of our lives and our society must be pruned in order for us to bear good fruit. We would need to be transformed. Jesus would be victorious, conquering as the Messiah, but his victory would attack the root of all sin and death in the world.

CONCLUSION

The fourth verse of "O Come, O Come Emmanuel" gives us another image for talking about the arrival of the Messiah: the branch of Jesse. Drawing on the promise to King David that God would make a king to reign forever from his line over Israel, we traced the development of this tree image in the Old Testament. From the thriving of David's kingdom to the desolation of the exile, the hope for a future Davidic king was seen as the emergence of a new branch from the stump of Jesse. Israel longed for the tree to bloom again, for God's king to emerge like a shoot breaking through the hardened winter earth. The birth narratives of Matthew and Luke are emphatic in connecting Jesus to this Davidic kingship. Jesus is the Messiah, born in the house of Jesse. He will reign forever on David's throne. Yet, with the arrival of this Messiah, the defeat of Israel's enemies was transformed. For God addressed the root of all evil, sin, and wickedness in the world through this child born to Mary. True victory, deliverance, and salvation would come not at the hands of power, but in the willing death of God's own Son.

DISCUSSION QUESTIONS FOR CHAPTER 4

1. The seed is often different from the tree. Can you think of other examples of items where the start is different from the result? How does this shape the way we understand Jesus' relationship to the Old Testament promises of a Messiah?

2. What is the meaning of "Messiah" in the Old Testament and how does it fit into Israel's story? How is this different from how you normally hear the term used?

3. How does the Old Testament develop the language of anointing, sonship, and kingship into a messianic hope? Can you think of examples where these same images show up to describe Jesus in the New Testament?

4. This chapter uses the example of racism to show the connection between individual sin and the larger structures of sin in our world. Can you think of other examples?

5. What does it mean for Jesus to be King in your life today? How can you remember this truth this Advent season?

5

The Key and the Door

O come, O Key of David, come
And open wide our heavenly home.
Make safe for us the heavenward road
And bar the way to death's abode.

On that day I will call my servant Eliakim son of Hilkiah,
and will clothe him with your robe and bind your sash on
him. I will commit your authority to his hand, and he shall
be a father to the inhabitants of Jerusalem and to the house
of Judah. I will place on his shoulder the key of the house of
David; he shall open, and no one shall shut; he shall shut, and
no one shall open. I will fasten him like a peg in a secure place,
and he will become a throne of honor to his ancestral house.
And they will hang on him the whole weight of his ancestral
house, the offspring and issue, every small vessel, from the cups
to all the flagons. On that day, says the LORD of hosts, the peg
that was fastened in a secure place will give way; it will be cut
down and fall, and the load that was on it will perish, for the
LORD has spoken. (Isa 22:20–25)

These are the words of the holy one, the true one,
who has the key of David,
who opens and no one will shut,
who shuts and no one opens (Rev 3:7b)

ON LOST KEYS AND CLOSED DOORS

Keys and doors are designed to provide safety and security. But often, they prove more of a headache than a help. Just ask anyone who has ever been locked out of their house or their car, and they will tell you how inconvenient keys can be. Door are also frustrating, especially if they are used primarily to exclude others. One of the slogans of the United Methodist Church is "Open Hearts, Open Minds, Open Doors." The slogan emphasizes the warm welcome that Methodist churches ought to extend to all people regardless of race, class, nationality, political view, or any other distinguishing mark of identity. But if you go by Methodist churches most days of the week, you will find that the doors are locked. You might even have to ring the doorbell or buzzer in order to go inside. And that's only if someone is there. If there is no one at the church, the church is probably locked up tight without a way to get in. That's true for the conservative and the liberal churches in the denomination. So much for open doors! I jest a little bit, but the point is worth noting. Our churches might have metaphorically open doors, but our actual doors are often locked. After all, we need the doors and the locks to provide safety and security. Speaking from experience as a pastor of a local Methodist church, I have had to change the locks on the church doors and repair shattered windows that were broken to gain access to the church. The locks and the doors are there to provide a sense of comfort, safety, and security. Both open doors and locked doors have their place.

And yet, as a parishioner once explained to me, "Locks will only keep out an honest thief." Locks, after all, can be picked. Most doors can be kicked in. Windows can be smashed to unlock doors. Our locks and doors give us a sense of safety and security, but they are a rather paltry security measure in the grand scheme of things.

Indeed, to many people, closed and locked doors are actually more of an invitation. They are a call to arms to push the boundaries. Activists against exclusion often oppose such "closed doors" by challenging the status quo. Such activism sometimes challenges us to be more like Christ in the world by welcoming all. But this desire to break down doors also reflects the fact that we often have a hard time with limits and barriers. We like to break world records, to push ourselves to personal bests, to defy the odds. When we encounter a barrier, we like to kick the door in or pick the lock.

But locks and closed doors are not always a bad thing. I remember coming home from school one day with my parents. As we pulled into the garage, our front-door windows were smashed in. There was a neighbor sitting in the garage, her arm cut and bleeding from trying to break into the house. She was a recovering alcoholic and had a deep craving for a drink that afternoon. She had come to our house to try and break in and get a drink. The windows, the door, and the locks had prevented her from getting in. They had prevented her from a terrible relapse. Perhaps they had saved her life. Sometimes our desire to get rid of doors and locks, to push ourselves to the limits, lead us to forget that the limits are important. We need boundaries to protect ourselves and others. Indeed, it is often the barriers themselves which give us freedom. All of this calls for wisdom and discernment. Locked doors might be a reminder of human limitation, but they also might be an act of injustice.

The complexities of doors, locks, and keys all stand in the background of the central image of the next verse of "O Come, O Come Emmanuel," where Jesus is described as the "Key of David" who unlocks humanity's return to God and bars the path to death and destruction. There is a double meaning emphasized here that highlights both the locking and unlocking work of Christ. As the key of David, Jesus both unlocks and locks simultaneously. The goal of this chapter is to grasp this door and key metaphor and see how the Advent hymn uses these images to instruct the church.

THE KEY OF DAVID

There are only two passages in the whole of the Bible that reference the "key of David." The first is found in the prophet Isaiah. Following an oracle that warns of the coming destruction of Jerusalem, Isaiah turns his prophetic rebuke to a rather minor character named Shebna (Isa 22:15). Shebna is a steward of the king of Judah, likely one of the king's advisors responsible for helping the king maintain order in the country. The Assyrian army had recently destroyed the Northern Kingdom of Israel and was bearing down on the Southern Kingdom of Judah. With war right at their doorstep, Shebna goes out to inspect the new tomb that he has recently built in the city. Shebna is unconcerned about the coming possibility of destruction and is only focused on his own legacy as reflected in this elaborate tomb (Isa 22:16–17). The word of God comes to Isaiah to rebuke Shebna for his disgraceful actions, with God declaring that Shebna will be removed from his post. Prophets often speak words of challenge, especially to those in power who have failed to use their power for practices of justice and righteousness. Shebna is targeted here for his unfaithfulness as an advisor to the king and is threatened with impending judgment.

But prophets also speak words of hope, often hand in hand with their words of God's judgment. Even though God punishes Israel, God does not forget God's people but maintains steadfast love for them. Following on the heels of the oracle against Shebna, Isaiah proclaims that his position will be taken by another. Eliakim will take Shebna's place. He will wear his robe and take his position as a steward of the house of Judah in Jerusalem. It is at this point that Isaiah introduces the language of the key: "I will place on his shoulder the key of the house of David; he shall open, and no one shut; he shall shut and no one shall open" (Isa 22:22). Eliakim is Shebna's replacement and receives all of his authority as the keeper of the key. Now, one should not imagine a tiny key on a key ring here. In the ancient world, this would be a large key (so large it was kept on one's shoulder, as the verse explains). This key would be used to lock and unlock the doors of the palace. This key gave Eliakim significant authority in the house of David, second only to the king himself. He controlled the entrances and exits of the palace. The key functions as a literal sign of Eliakim's new power and control in the palace and as a metaphor for his role as second-in-command.

This role reversal seems to have coincided with a moment of hope for the people of Judah and the house of David in Jerusalem. As Eliakim is promoted, the impending invasion of Assyria is thwarted by King Hezekiah and his advisors. God intervenes to save Jerusalem from the Assyrians (2 Kgs 18–19). For a short time, King Hezekiah and his advisor Eliakim are able to lock out the destructive forces. Unfortunately, that victory is short-lived, as the Southern Kingdom of Judah is later captured by the Babylonians and led into exile. Still, the reference to the key of David is here connected to a transfer of power and authority from one person to another. Its association with the house of David invokes the promise made to David by God of a king that would reign forever in David's line. The metaphorical power of the key creates a messianic image.

The second use of the key of David in the Bible comes in the book of Revelation, the final book in the New Testament. The seer John has been exiled to the island of Patmos, where he receives a vision of the risen and exalted Lord, Jesus the Messiah. Jesus gives John a special revelation that he is told to send to seven churches in Asia Minor. The word for revelation can also be translated as "apocalypse" (in Greek, *apokalupsis*), hence why people often use "Apocalypse" as the title for the book of Revelation. "Revelation" and "apocalypse" are synonyms. However, the modern meaning of apocalypse as the destructive end of the world is misleading in this context. While Revelation has some things to say about the future (especially Jesus' return in glory), the term "apocalypse" used to describe John's book is actually better understood as a revealing or unveiling of God's power. An apocalypse uncovers what God is doing behind the scenes of history. An apocalypse reminds people that God is in charge. Despite how hopeless the world appears, God will return to fix what is broken. Understanding an apocalypse is like the scene in the *Wizard of Oz* where Dorothy is marveling before the great and power Oz only to have Toto reveal that it is all an illusion operated by a man behind a curtain. John's apocalypse pulls back the curtain on the evil and wickedness of the world to show that God is ultimately in control. God will bring the future to completion with the return of Christ. The message of Revelation is meant to inspire its readers to continue to be faithful in their witness, enduring the hardships and suffering in this world because they have the sure hope that God's future will come. For its earliest readers in the Roman Empire who faced opposition, the continual pressure to abandon their beliefs in Jesus to better fit in with their pagan neighbors, and the complacency that comes with prosperity, Revelation was a wake-up call to inspire faithful living.

Part of the message of Revelation consists of several short letters addressed to specific churches in Asia Minor. The letters offer comfort to the churches in their hardships, and they also rebuke their disobedience. One of these letters is addressed to the church in Philadelphia (a city in Asia Minor—modern-day Turkey—not Philadelphia, Pennsylvania). It begins: "These are the words of the holy one, the true one, who has the key of David, who opens and no one will shut, who shuts and no one opens" (Rev 3:7). Revelation draws quite deliberately on the oracle to Eliakim in Isa 22, but has now applied the imagery to Jesus the Messiah. This is seen not only in the use of the expression "key of David" but also in the authority that comes with that key to open and shut, just as was assigned to Eliakim in Isa 22:22.

But what exactly does it mean for Jesus to have this key? The image of the key is not here used in a literal sense, as if Jesus can open the palace doors like Eliakim. Rather, it is its symbolic force that Revelation claims for Jesus. Jesus has the authority associated with the key. This is a royal authority (hence the association with David) because Jesus himself is the Messiah from the line of David. As Revelation explains elsewhere, Jesus is the conquering Lion of Judah, the Root of David (Rev 5:5), and for this reason he has all authority on heaven and earth. But there is another important image that is communicated by the metaphor of the key. With this authority that Jesus has, he is also able to open and to shut. Throughout Revelation, this opening and shutting authority is expressed in various ways. Jesus alone can open the scroll that unfolds God's future (Rev 5:5). Likewise, the second coming of Jesus results in the shutting up of Satan, that ancient serpent, in the pit (Rev 20:1–3).

These examples depict a rather cosmic view of Jesus' authority, as he has power over all things in heaven and on earth. But the same authority can also be depicted in individual circumstances. For the church in Philadelphia, Jesus has opened a door for them in the face of their persecution. Despite worldly rejection, Jesus is able to open the door for them which no one else can shut.

From this perspective, we can begin to understand the imagery of the key of David in "O Come, O Come Emmanuel." The Advent hymn prays for the arrival of the key of David, the one who has authority over all things. The double vision of Advent is particularly important with this image, as the appeal to the key refers not just to Jesus' arrival as a child but also to his second coming. Through his birth, death, and resurrection, Jesus has been given all authority in heaven and on earth, the key to the unfolding of God's promises for the future (Matt 28:18–25). The fullness of this authority will be expressed when he returns in glory and every knee bows before him (Phil 2:10–11). But what does this authority mean for Christ's followers? To understand this, we have to delve even deeper into our key imagery.

LOCKING AND UNLOCKING

Once one has grasped the image of Jesus as the key of David, there are other passages that gravitate to the image that help us understand Jesus' authority as the one who can open and shut. As the Advent hymn encourages us to see, the image of the key reveals Jesus' power to bar the way that leads to death and open wide the path that leads to heaven's home. Already in that beautiful image, we are taken back into the language of exile and return with the words of Isaiah the prophet rattling in our ears as he calls for the way to be prepared for God's return (Isa 40:4–5). At the start of each of the Gospels, John the Baptist comes to prepare the people for God's return, echoing that promise of Isaiah. But what follows on the heels of John's proclamation is not the arrival of God in glory but the introduction of Jesus of Nazareth. As the early Christians came to understand it, the coming of Jesus was the coming of God to earth. His arrival paved the way for all humanity to return back to God. His arrival unlocked the path back to God's presence. The key imagery, the locking and unlocking, is one way of understanding Jesus' purpose in the world.

Consider another reflection of this theme in the various exorcisms that Jesus performs. Jesus often confronts people hounded by unclean spirits that are destroying their lives. But his encounters with these spirits are always an opportunity for him to display his power. He rebukes the spirits and casts them out of the person. He unbinds people from oppression even as he binds the evil forces. There is a sort of locking and unlocking going on here. When asked about his exorcisms, Jesus also points toward the locking and unlocking metaphor: "But no one can enter a strong man's house and plunder his property without first tying up the strong man; then indeed the house can be plundered" (Mark 3:27). Jesus has power to tie up wickedness and loose the oppressed. Jesus understands his ministry as initiating a conflict with the forces of evil exemplified by Satan and the wicked spirits. With each exorcism, he is locking up the ways of wickedness in anticipation of the ultimate defeat of evil at the end of days.

A similar display of Jesus' authority to lock and unlock is seen in the various healing miracles. Jesus brings healing into individuals' lives in the same way that he performs his exorcisms. He has authority to heal the sick, restore the broken, and remove the stigmas attached to the various ailments that leave individuals bound in suffering. For instance, Jesus can rebuke a fever that leaves Peter's mother-in-law bedridden (Matt 8:14–17). Both the exorcisms and the healing miracles in the Gospels are ways of communicating Jesus' power and authority. He has come to bind and to loose, to lock and unlock. He is the key of David.

Jesus also bestows this authority in his name to those who follow him. Already in his ministry, the disciples are given authority by Jesus to cast out the evil spirits and heal the sick as his representatives (Matt 10:1). This theme of authority imparted to the followers of Jesus regularly shows up in the Gospels, often with a related use of the theme of unlocking and locking. After Simon Peter confesses that Jesus is the Christ, Jesus declares that Simon's name will be

Peter, for he will be the rock, the foundation, of the church. Peter will become a major leader of the early church and a central pillar in its proclamation to the Jews and the Gentiles (cf. Acts 2–15). But Jesus continues by describing the authority that will be given to Peter and the church he builds: "I will give you the keys of the kingdom of heaven, and whatever you bind on earth will be bound in heaven, and whatever you loose on earth will be loosed in heaven" (Matt 16:19). This promise should immediately remind us of the key imagery of Isaiah. Here, Jesus is passing on the promise of Eliakim as the keeper of the key to Peter and the church. Jesus' followers will have authority to open and shut in the world as they resist evil and liberate the oppressed in his name. A similar promise is given at the end of the Gospel of Matthew, where Jesus is given all authority and subsequently empowers the disciples to go out to do this work with confidence. But Matt 16:19 is striking because it takes the words of the prophet Isaiah and has them transmitted through Jesus to Peter as representative of the church. So we ought to ask: Who has the key of David here—is it Jesus, or is it the church?

This takes us right to the heart of an essential theme of Advent. The arrival of God in the flesh as Jesus the Messiah means that Jesus is both fully God and fully man. He shares fully in the divine identity, but is also perfectly human. Because he stands in the gap between humans and God, he is able to repair the divide between the two. Humanity is invited to be joined with Christ, to share in Christ, in order to be lifted and reconciled back to God. As Paul explains, Christ is the head and the church is the body (Col 1:18). We are united to the head and guided by the head. It is this idea that lies behind the sharing of the key between Christ and the church. Jesus has been given all authority, and he passes that authority on to his followers. He is the key of David, and he gives the key of heaven to the church, his followers on earth.

In the early 1990s, there was a movement in Christianity marked by the wearing of WWJD bracelets, an acronym that poses the question "What would Jesus do?" On one level, this is always a fitting question for the church to ask itself as it seeks to follow Jesus in the world. We all have room to grow in obedience in following Jesus. We can all grow in following where he leads in our lives, communities, and the world. But on another level, that question is inexact. The question should not be "What would Jesus do?" but rather "What is Jesus doing?" For Jesus still reigns as Lord. As Revelation declares, he is still unlocking and locking doors. He is still locking the way of death and opening the way of heaven. Christ has not stopped working. Rather, he has invited the church to join in that ongoing work already underway in our world. The church lays claim to the keys of the kingdom because it is joined to the key of David, who still reigns in power and authority. Learning to walk in the authority given by Christ means learning to keep up with Christ's work in the world.

THE DOOR AND THE WAY

This leads us to the extension of the metaphor of the key of David in our Advent hymn. "O Come, O Come Emmanuel" does not simply talk about Jesus as the one with authority on earth and heaven. Rather, the image of the key is used to lay out a contrast between two competing paths in the world. Jesus bars the path of death and shuts the door on wickedness even as he opens up the way that leads to our heavenly home. The Advent hymn is trying to help us understand that Jesus' authority is not some arbitrary power that does whatever it wants. Rather, Jesus has come to lay out a specific path.

There is a long-standing tradition in Jewish and Christian Scripture called "the two ways." It is a contrast between two ways of life laid out before humanity. Every person must choose which path to walk. There is a way that leads to life through obedience to God, and there is a way that leads to death. The image of the two ways is set forth in Deuteronomy, where, after recounting the law God gives Israel to follow, Israel is given a decision to choose between the two ways of obedience and disobedience: "See, I have set before you today life and prosperity, death and destruction" (Deut 30:15). A similar tradition lies behind the book of Proverbs with its contrast between the way of wisdom that leads to life and the way of the fool that leads to destruction. Jesus and the earliest

Christians used this exact same imagery to talk about the Christian life. It is a life of obedience to God and commitment to Christ. Jesus describes his teaching as a contrast between two ways: a difficult way of obedience with a narrow gate and the wide road that leads to destruction (Matt 7:13–14). Indeed, before Christianity was even called "Christianity," it was called "the Way," capturing the idea that Christianity lays out a specific way of life, a way that leads to life (Acts 9:2). Christianity proclaims that there is a way that that lies open to us that leads us back to God.

These two ways only further deepen the metaphor of Jesus as the key of David. For he has unlocked the door that leads to a specific way. He opens the door that leads to life eternal in the presence of God and locks the door of death. Our Advent hymn drops us right down in the midst of these two ways in order to declare that Jesus as the key of David has locked the door on one way and unlocked the path on the other. As Jesus declares in John's Gospel, he is both the gate and the way. Jesus is "the way, the truth, and the life" (John 14:6). He is the gate through which the sheep enter into salvation (John 10:9). Through his ministry, death, and resurrection, Jesus has opened wide the way of life and barred the way of death. The two paths preached throughout the Bible all hinge on the authority of Christ to open the way of life and bar the way of death. The key of David unlocks and locks.

CONCLUSION

The fifth verse of "O Come, O Come Emmanuel" introduces us to what at first appears a rather insignificant title: Jesus as the key of David. While used only briefly in Isaiah and Revelation, the idea behind that metaphor quickly becomes a rich and evocative image. What starts as a declaration of Jesus' authority leads us to explore the authority that Christ has passed on to the church. Like a match dropped on dry wood, the image of Jesus as the key of David is a small spark that quickly creates a beautiful fire that invites us to come close to warm ourselves.

DISCUSSION QUESTIONS FOR CHAPTER 5

1. What are some of the dangers of locks and doors? What are some of the benefits? Do you find yourself more attracted to shutting and locking doors or kicking down locked doors?
2. What does the image of Jesus as a key suggest to you? What does he unlock or lock in your life?
3. How does the image of locking and unlocking help us understand Jesus' ministry in the Gospels? How does it relate to the church's ongoing work?
4. In what ways can the church walk in the authority of Jesus through practices of locking and unlocking?
5. What does it mean today to think of the two ways—the ways of life and death—in a world where there are so many competing options? Does everything either fit into one way or the other?

6

The Star in the Darkness

O come, O Bright and Morning Star,
and bring us comfort from afar!
Dispel the shadows of the night
and turn our darkness into light.

The oracle of Balaam son of Beor,
    the oracle of the man whose eye is clear,
the oracle of one who hears the words of God,
    and knows the knowledge of the Most High,
who sees the vision of the Almighty,
    who falls down, but with his eyes uncovered:
I see him, but not now;
    I behold him, but not near—
a star shall come out of Jacob,
    and a scepter shall rise out of Israel;
it shall crush the borderlands of Moab,
    and the territory of all the Shethites.
Edom will become a possession,
    Seir a possession of its enemies,
    while Israel does valiantly.

One out of Jacob shall rule,
and destroy the survivors of Ir. (Num 24:15–19)

In the time of King Herod, after Jesus was born in Bethlehem
of Judea, wise men from the East came to Jerusalem, asking,
"Where is the child who has been born king of the Jews? For
we observed his star at its rising, and have come to pay him
homage." (Matt 2:1–2)

LOOK TO THE STARS

The most exciting day of elementary school, with the exception of
the last day of school before the summer, was the day that we got
to go to the Star Lab. The Star Lab was a giant, inflatable gray dome
set up in the library. We would have to take off our shoes to climb
through the tiny tunnel into the inflated dome. Once inside, we
would sit along the walls and look up to the domed roof, where the
teacher would project stars and point out the various constellations
with a laser pointer. The teacher would trace the constellations and
tell the stories of the myths behind them. This fascinated me as a
child. I loved hearing about Orion and Cassiopeia as I found the
cluster of stars that make up Orion's Belt or the outline of the Big
Dipper. There was something exciting about looking at the stars
and having them tell a story. It gave me a sense of wonder to think
I was part of this grand story written on the very stars themselves.

Of course, I grew up and came to realize that the myths about
the constellations were just stories made up over time and passed
down from generation to generation. But that hasn't stopped me
from looking to the stars and wanting them to tell a story. And
I'm not alone. This longing can be found in our language and in
our practices. We can speak of "star-crossed lovers," borrowing the
Shakespearean phrase for the unhappy fate of lost love. We also see
the practices of astrology that show up in the horoscopes of news-
papers and magazines. Some think that being born under a certain
set of stars, an astrological sign like Sagittarius or Gemini, shapes
our mood, our luck, and our future. But even beyond these popular

superstitions, humans have often connected their lives to the stars. Noted astrophysicist Neil deGrasse Tyson, who would mock the absurdity of astrology as betraying the insights of modern science, nevertheless can claim in his *Astrophysics for People in a Hurry* that "we are stardust brought to life, then empowered by the universe to figure itself out and we have only just begun."[1] While the astrophysicist is making a scientific point (we are made up of the same material as the stars), he is also suggesting a more romantic claim—that there is somehow a purpose that ties us to the stars, that humans as stardust come to life are trying to figure things out. This goes beyond astrophysics to something deeper about what it means to be human. It is the sense one gets when standing in front of a vast sky of stars. It is simultaneously a feeling of being utterly insignificant and yet also utterly important. As the psalmist declares, "What are human beings that you are mindful of them, mortals that you care for them? Yet you have made them a little lower than God, and crowned them with glory and honor" (Ps 8:4–5).

The fifth verse of "O Come, O Come Emmanuel" also invites us to look to the stars. But we are invited not just to gaze into the vastness of space. We are to look for a specific star, the bright and morning star, who has come to guide us out of the darkness and into the light of God. Like that familiar star that rises in the morning to dispel the night, we are invited to look to Christ as the star that casts aside the darkness. But the image of the star also tells an important story, rooted in Israel's scriptures, that leads us further on our Advent journey together.

A STAR OUT OF JACOB

One of the earliest significant references we have to stars in Israel's scriptures comes in the story of Abraham in Gen 12–25. His story begins when he is named Abram while still living in the land of Ur of the Chaldeans, a place where multiple gods are worshiped. (Gen 11:31–32). But then Abram receives a call from the one true God. God asks him to pack up shop and leave his home and his

1. Tyson, *Astrophysics*, 15.

extended family to follow God to a land God will show him. This radical call to trust and obey God is joined with a promise. God will make Abram a great nation, bless him, and make him a blessing to the nations (Gen 12:1–3). The call to Abram launches his story of commitment to God and begins a new chapter in God's plan to rescue and redeem the world. The God who created all things chooses Abram as a partner in the salvation of the nations.

But the journey to follow God to a new land is not easy. His story is filled with ups and downs. Abram does not become the father of faith overnight. He often refuses to trust God, tries to fulfill God's promises on his own, and struggles to be obedient. Yet, despite the challenges, he persists in his commitment to God. One night during his journey, God comes to Abram in a vision to encourage him not to be afraid. Abram is concerned about his future. He has left his family behind, and he and his wife, do not have any kids. When they die, their name will die with them. There is no heir to their name, land, or family heritage (Gen 15:1–3). So God makes a promise to Abram. He tells Abram to go out and look at the stars spread across the night sky: "Look toward heaven and count the stars," God says. "So shall your descendants be." At that moment, Abram believes God, and it is "reckoned it to him as righteousness" (Gen 15:5–6). The moment of Abram's belief—his trust in and obedience to God—is tied to the counting of the stars. The stars become a reminder that God will give Abram descendants too numerous to count.

Sure enough, over time, Abram becomes Abraham, a name that means "father of the people," a fitting change as his descendants grow and spread. Abraham has a son named Isaac. Isaac has two sons, Esau and Jacob. Jacob, who is renamed "Israel," has twelve sons, who become the heads of the twelve tribes of Israel. The God of Abraham, Isaac, and Jacob is keeping the promise. Generation by generation, more and more "stars" are born to Abraham's family. Israel is often reminded of their chosen status by an appeal to the promise of Abraham, for the people multiply like the stars, just as God promised (Deut 1:10; 1 Chron 27:23). Stars become a metaphor for the people of Israel.

But the star image does not remain isolated to a description of Israel alone. It also becomes associated with the Messiah, the anointed ruler from the line of David. How does that happen? On one hand, this sort of replacement of the part for the whole is common in the Bible. It is a literary technique called synecdoche. Consider the aphorism "The pen is mightier than the sword." The terms "pen" and "sword" are replacements for the broader realities "writing" and "war." The part replaces the whole. We have already seen synecdoche at work with some of our biblical images. Just as Israel can be God's son, so the king is also God's son, since the king is the part that stands in for the whole. The king represents the whole people, so there is synecdoche at work in the expression. Images of Israel as the people of God often overlap with images of their ruling king (or future messianic leader). So if Israel as a people are as numerous as the stars, it is no surprise that their king might also be associated with a star.

On the other hand, in ancient prophecy, there is particular importance in the metaphor of the star as an image of the coming Messiah. The origin of that image is found in the book of Numbers, a book that sounds about exciting as *Book of Spreadsheets*. But nestled between Numbers' description of the census of Israelites after the Exodus and the rules for their sacrificial offerings, the book contains a number of fascinating stories about Israel's challenges on its way to the promised land. One of them involves a prophet named Balaam, who is hired by Balak, king of the Moabites, to curse the Israelites. Balak has seen other nations fall to Israel, and he is afraid that his people are next. So he decides to get some supernatural help and hires Balaam to speak curses over the Israelites. There is only one problem. Every time Balaam tries to open his mouth to curse the Israelites, he can only speak blessings upon Balak's opponents. The one God, the God of Israel, does not let Balaam curse the Israelites.

In one of these attempted curses-turned-blessings, Balaam utters a prophecy about a star: "I see him, but not now; I behold him, but not near—a star shall come out of Jacob and a scepter shall rise out of Israel" (Num 24:17). The prophetic oracle is a promise of a coming ruler, described as a scepter and a star, who will arise from Israel and crush their opponents. Balaam projects this into the future ("I see him, but not now . . ."). This image correlates nicely with many of the other messianic promises in the Hebrew Bible. A coming ruler-king who would defeat Israel's enemies seems to point toward a Messiah. And so, alongside the root of Jesse and Emmanuel, the Star of Jacob became an image for God's Messiah in the Old Testament.

THE MESSIANIC STAR

The image of the messianic star became particularly powerful for the ancient Jews in the centuries leading up to Jesus. But as is often the case with Israel's ancient prophecies, the meaning was subject to competing interpretations. Who did this star image best describe? The evidence from ancient Judaism shows how many different figures became associated with this prophetic hope.

In one of the Dead Sea Scrolls, the Qumran community interprets Num 24:17 as a prediction of the Messiah, perhaps a person known to their own community.[2] The Dead Sea Scrolls were written a few centuries before Jesus and reveal a group of Jews anxious about the future of Israel. The Numbers prophecy became a way for the people of the Qumran community to talk about their own leadership and separation from the rest of the Jewish people. Perhaps the star of Jacob was a leader known to them?

Josephus, a Jewish historian writing in the first century CE, also offers an interpretation of the oracle of Balaam based on his own experience. He saw the Roman general Vespasian's victory over Palestine, followed by Vespasian's ascension to the role of Roman emperor. Did this fulfill the prophecies of a coming star?[3] While many of his fellow Jews rejected the idea that a Roman leader would be the promised deliverer, Josephus found this interpretation to his liking (not least because he was working for the Romans).

There is also the example of Simon ben Kosevah, later called Bar Kokhba because *kokhba* is Hebrew for "star." Simon led a revolt against the Romans from 132–35 CE, during which time he

2. 4Q175.
3. Josephus, *Jewish War*, 6:288–312.

declared himself a prince of the people. Simon was regarded as a possible messiah and called the "son of the star." His supporters were associating him with the oracle of Balaam from Num 24:17. Now, not all of the Jews of his day and age supported this interpretation. Many instead preferred to mock him with the name Simon bar Kozibah ("the son of the lie" in Hebrew) because they thought he was leading the Jewish people astray. While Simon's revolt was short-lived and he was eventually defeated by the Romans, the star imagery still expressed Jewish hopes.

What all of these examples show us is that the words of Israel's scriptures (especially Balaam's star oracle) exercised a powerful hold on the Jewish imagination. It was the resource from which Jews drew to understand and interpret the political events around them as they longed for God's deliverance. All three interpretations linked Balaam's image of the star to a possible messianic deliverer.

In the same way, the oracle was interpreted among the Christians to depict Jesus as the fulfillment of Israel's messianic expectations. It is no surprise that many of the New Testament writings associate Jesus with the star. Revelation 22:16, for instance, describes Jesus as the bright and morning star alongside his description as a descendant of David's line. The image of the Messiah as the star also seems to exert a magnetic pull on other images from the New Testament. As seen in the use of the star in Revelation, Jesus is also associated with a bright, shining light. He is not just any star, he is the star of a *new morning*. The imagery of light was readily at hand to capture the force of the messianic star. Just as the Messiah would defeat Israel's enemies, so the star's light would drive out the darkness.

This light imagery also resonates with Old Testament promises associated with the Messiah. The servant of Isa 49 would be "a light to the nations" so that God's salvation "may reach to the ends of the earth" (Isa 49:6). Or, the servant would be "a light to the nations, to open the eyes that are blind, to bring out the prisoners from the dungeon, from the prison those who sit in darkness" (Isa 42:6–7). God's coming light would mean the defeat of darkness in all its forms. The Messiah as a star of great light weaves all of this together into a complex image.

If those words or images sound familiar, it is probably because you have heard them in the Gospel accounts of Jesus. Stars and light intersect as they capture Israel's hopes about the Messiah. Time and again, the imagery of light and the star from the servant oracles of Isaiah are associated with Jesus and his ministry. At his birth, the prophet Simeon declares that Jesus will be "a light for revelation to the Gentiles and for glory to your people Israel" (Luke 3:32). In John 8:12, Jesus calls himself the "light of the world" because "whoever follows me will never walk in darkness but will have the light of life." Jesus clearly locates himself in the imagery of light and darkness and invokes the fulfillment of the messianic star imagery. According to Luke 4:16–21, Jesus stresses this connection himself when, after reading aloud from Isaiah in a synagogue, he says, "Today this scripture has been fulfilled in your hearing" (Luke 4:21).

It is this overlap of biblical promises that hangs behind the description in "O Come, O Come Emmanuel" of Jesus as the bright and morning star. The star is not just an image or a title, it is also a summary of Jesus' mission in the world. He comes, as the song declares, to "dispel the shadows of the night and turn our darkness into light." He comes with light to drive out the darkness. But unlike the rumors of other fulfillments of the star oracle circulating in Jesus' day, Jesus will not drive out the darkness with military might. The light of Christ penetrates deeper and drives out the darkness at the very core of the human heart. It fulfills God's purposes for the world laid out since Abraham first looked to the stars as a symbol of his descendants. Where Israel had failed to be a light, where the kings had each failed to be the coming star, Jesus would prove victorious. He would reveal God's glory to the world, even in the darkness of death. He would prove faithful and true. Although the whole world sat in darkness as the light was put out when the Messiah was crucified, from the empty tomb arose a new morning, a bright and morning star. Light shines in the darkness. The Sun has risen. The gospel is seen in the Star.

A STAR OVER BETHLEHEM AND
THE POLITICS OF CHRISTMAS

There is one other important passage where the Messiah and the star are brought together in the Gospels. In Matt 2, we hear the story of the magi, these wise men who arrive in Judea from the East in search of a star. They claim that their arrival is the result of seeing a star in the skies: "Where is the child who has been born king of the Jews? For we observed his star at its rising, and have come to pay him homage" (Matt 2:2). Wise men, or magi, were a sort of catch-all category to refer to advisors and officials who worked in the courts of royalty, especially in the areas of Persia, Babylon, and Parthia. They were known for their wisdom and their knowledge of more obscure things like astronomy/astrology, history, and magic. Picture Jafar from *Aladdin* and you have the right sort of idea. In this passage, the magi see a special star in the sky and follow it to Judea. They take the sign of the star as an omen of the birth of the king of the Jews. Assuming a royal birth, they jump to the conclusion that he will be found in the palace. But they are in for a surprise when the newborn king is not found there. Again, we have the combination of ideas we have seen from our exploration of the star image. There is the echo of the prophecy from Numbers, there is the association of the star with the king of the Jews, and there is the difficult struggle to know who this prophecy is about. The wise men react like so many others. They go to the place where you would expect a king. Like calling the leader of the Jewish revolt the "son of the star" or ascribing the star status to the Roman emperor, the wise men assume that the coming star must be a military leader or king living in the palace.

But the palace staff and King Herod are shocked by their arrival. They know nothing of this new king. King Herod calls together his scholars to figure out where this new king will be born. They point to the city of Bethlehem, citing the prophetic words of Mic 5:2. So the magi pack up and leave the palace to head toward Bethlehem, where this new king will be found. But before they leave, they promise to return to Herod after they find the king to let him know his whereabouts. After all, Herod has his own conniving plans for this "new king."

The wise men follow the star, for the star itself seems to be moving and leading them to the place where Jesus lies. Once there, they find a child in the arms of Mary, his mother. They react to this discovery by bowing down in worship of the child and offering gifts of gold, frankincense, and myrrh. The symbolic act of the foreign kings coming to bow before the child with gifts is itself an echo of the promise of Isaiah of the coming welcome of the Gentiles into the kingdom of God (Isa 60:6). This will not only be Israel's king. This will be the king of the whole world. The star has come as a light to all nations.

The emphasis on kingship also leads us to a major takeaway from the image of the star throughout Scripture, but especially in Matt 2. We should not lose sight of the fact that the star is a political symbol. It is a statement about God's coming king. The politics of Matthew are written into almost every line if we pay careful attention. First, the magi are political advisers. Their job revolves around politics, since they make their living advising kings and rulers. But the wise men have defected from their own kingdoms (wherever that may have been) to search for another king. They have journeyed from afar to find this king of the Jews. These wise men are looking for a political leader and have come to declare their allegiance to this new king.

Second, these wise men report to the king of Judea, Herod the Great, and ask about the new king. This adds another layer of political intrigue to the story, because this new king of the world they seek is not Herod himself. It is someone else born in his kingdom. Herod is not happy that there is a rival to his throne. After all, nothing upsets those in power more than being told that there is someone more powerful than them. When Herod is told that there is a new king in town, the real king of the Jews, it is like taking a needle to pop his inflated ego. The news infuriates Herod, so when Herod sends the wise men to Bethlehem, he asks them to tell him when they find the kid. For he plans to kill the one who threatens his power. When this plot of Herod fails, Herod takes matters into his own hands and slaughters all the boys under the age of two in the area (Matt 3:16–18). There are serious, even deadly, political consequences that follow the birth of Jesus the Messiah.

These points serve as a reminder that Jesus' messianic identity is a political claim. The true politics of Christmas, if you will, is heeding the call that Jesus is King and Lord. It is devoting one's allegiance to the Messiah born in a manger. Ultimately, this is what the wise men do. They have traveled from a far to meet the king, and when they meet the king, they bow before him. They submit, show reverence, and devote their allegiance. They declare their true political commitment.

Every year, there is a concern that is raised in the media about the "war on Christmas." There is a fear that Christ is being removed from Christmas. Every year without fail, the same concerns are sounded in some form or fashion, often among Christians themselves. But such a reaction is completely overblown. For the real politics of Christmas are seen in the actions of the wise men. The church's concern should not be how to keep Christ in the popular celebrations of Christmas. It should be helping Christians keep Christ at the forefront of their allegiance. This story reveals a basic truth about the politics of Christmas. The claim that Jesus is the king of the Jews and God's chosen Messiah for the world brings a challenge to all other powers. There is one star and one king. The wise men make a choice about who will rule in their lives, and they invite us to do the same. Every holiday season—indeed, every day—we are invited to live as those bowed before our savior.

After all, what is it that is so shocking about the birth of Jesus, the political claim of Christmas, that incited Herod to violence? What has Jesus done or said politically to generate such hatred? Nothing yet! Jesus is just a baby in a manger. He is not stirring up resistance, speaking out against any policy of Herod, or gathering his own militia. Rather, it is the claim made by God and others about Jesus as the coming Messiah that Herod sees as a threat. It is the star that proclaims his birth that acts as a warning notice for all other kings and authorities. It is the star's meaning that throws Herod into such a violent rage. For Herod knows that if Jesus is the true king from God, there will be judgment on his own reign.

This leads us to the true paradox of Matt 2. For where is the king found? Where does the star lead? It does not lead to the palaces or the military encampments. The true King of Israel is not found among the wealthy and the elite. He is not found among the strong and powerful. He is not a Roman general or Jewish rebel leader. The true King is found in the arms of a Jewish woman. And his kingdom will be enacted outside the standard political forces of power, might, and wealth. This King will live by a love that dies for friend and enemy alike. He will give people the hope that God has come and is rescuing the world. He will give people joy because light has emerged in the darkness. He will be the bright and morning star that casts out the darkness and shadow of death. That is the politics that the magi sign up for, and it is the invitation to allegiance that Jesus extends to us today. Look to the true Star, enter into the Light, and live as those committed to the coming King of the world.

CONCLUSION

The sixth verse of "O Come, O Come Emmanuel" invites us to look to the stars to see if we might catch a glimpse of God's promises among us. As we follow the image of the star, we move from otherworldly heavenly gazing to the very earthly political realities of first-century Judaism. The star, although rooted in God's promise to Abraham, quickly became a symbol for Israel's hopes for a messianic leader who would drive out God's opponents and bring God's kingdom of glory on earth. The earliest Christians also used the image to describe Jesus, drawing on Jesus' own description of his ministry as the dawning of a new light. They told the story of the star that shown over Bethlehem at Jesus' birth, declaring to the world that God's Messiah had come. It was a heavenly sign of an earthly reality. The political meaning of the symbol was not lost on them, for the star at Jesus' birth was seen as a political threat to King Herod. Yet, Jesus also redefined the political force of the star imagery. For his life, death, and resurrection did not create a political revolution. Instead, they launched something deeper and more significant. For Jesus brings a light that casts out the darkness, or, as the hymn declares, "dispels the shadows of night." While this is revolutionary, it looks different than what we might expect. Jesus the Messiah tackles the depths of sin and despair, he confronts injustice and oppression in all of its forms, and through his ministry of peace and his sacrificial death, he defeats the darkness with the brightest of lights. With his resurrection, a new age emerges, bursting forth from the tomb like the dawn of a new era. Christ is the bright and morning star.

DISCUSSION QUESTIONS FOR CHAPTER 6

1. What do you feel when you look at the stars? Do you feel like you are part of a bigger story or that you are insignificant before the grandeur of the heavens?
2. What are the various meanings of the star in the story of Israel in the Old Testament? How does it function as a kind of synecdoche?
3. How was the star interpreted by Jews around the time of Jesus? Where did they agree and disagree?
4. How is the star image used to describe Jesus in the New Testament? How does it show up in the Christmas story?
5. What does political allegiance to Jesus look like today? How do we declare him as King in the twenty-first century?

7

The Desire of Nations

O come, O King of nations, bind
in one the hearts of all mankind.
Bid all our sad divisions cease
and be yourself our King of Peace.

And I will shake all nations, and the desire of all nations shall
come: and I will fill this house with glory, saith the LORD of
hosts. (Hag 2:7 KJV)

In days to come
    the mountain of the LORD's house
shall be established as the highest of the mountains,
    and shall be raised above the hills;
all the nations shall stream to it. (Isa 2:2)

Guided by the Spirit, Simeon came into the temple; and when
the parents brought in the child Jesus, to do for him what was
customary under the law, Simeon took him in his arms and
praised God, saying,
"Master, now you are dismissing your servant in peace,
    according to your word;

for my eyes have seen your salvation,
   which you have prepared in the presence of all peoples,
a light for revelation to the Gentiles
   and for glory to your people Israel." (Luke 2:27–33)

ALL NATIONS UNDER GOD

I knew Memorial Day was not a good time to bring up the subject. But the words of the mayor at the morning service of remembrance were simply misleading. Even worse, they bordered on the blasphemous. So as my family gathered for lunch that afternoon, I decided to open the can of worms. Like Jeremiah, I had a word in me that was a like a fire in my bones I simply had to proclaim. I cleared my throat and started in, "You know, God doesn't just bless America. God is also the God of all the nations, even the nations that make war with America." Let the argument begin.

The event that launched this declaration and the argument that followed was my family's attendance at the local Memorial Day event on the town square. As a Boy Scout, I had been a part of the service every year since I could remember. I served in the color guard as we brought the flags in for the event, or I helped with the other scouts to place tiny American flags next to the names of those who had lost their lives in past wars. The service was solemn. In our small town, many of the persons who would gather on that day could remember the individuals who had served and given their lives in WWII, Korea, and Vietnam. It was still a fresh memory. Those memorialized were family: parents, children, grandparents, descendants. After the reading of the fallen soldiers' names, it was customary for the village mayor to share a few words.

But when the mayor took the podium that day, what followed was a jumbled bunch of clichés with vague theological claims that presented a distorted view of God, Jesus Christ, and the Bible. The mayor declared how blessed America was by God, how the United States stood for the godly values of the Bible, and how our success in battle showed America's chosen status by God. The nations who opposed us had all learned from the hands of our soldiers that our nation was committed to freedom. Americans were willing to die for freedom. And these nations had since come over to our side. God had blessed America to save the world.

Perhaps this had always been how the Memorial Day service proceeded and I had never recognized it before. But this year, I was a different person with a different perspective. I had just returned from a prayer trip to a small country in North Africa, where I had been visiting and worshiping with a small group of Christians that were trying to survive in a predominantly Muslim country. I heard of the suffering they faced as they converted to Christianity, suffering often inflicted by their communities and families. I listened as they described having to worship in hiding, how they hid their Bibles lest they be found and confiscated. Through it all, these few Christians praised the God who had saved them in Jesus Christ, who gave them strength and courage to love their enemies. This was a Christianity I had never known before, a Christianity completely removed from the trappings of American culture. There were no big churches on the corner. There were no youth groups with their conferences pulsing with loud guitars. There were no Christian bookstores or worship-music radio stations. Christianity had been stripped down to its life-giving essentials: a deep trust in Christ, a hunger for Scripture, courage and faith grounded in the one God. But despite how different this church was from my church back home, I clearly saw the fruit of the Spirit. I knew I was united to these believers as brothers and sisters in Christ. God was not the God of America only. God was also the God of the nations. If anything, all the trappings of American Christianity that resulted from its fusion with civil religion and consumerism had hidden an important element of the church that I had never considered. The church is universal. It is global. God is the God of all the nations. With all of the zeal of this new insight, I came home and decided to share my insights with my family on Memorial Day.

The final verse of our Advent hymn challenges us with a similar universal view of the church. It opens with a powerful reminder that Christ is the King of nations. All the nations. Full stop. As the Advent hymn comes to an end, we are reminded of the universal Christ and the plan of God for the whole created order. The image of the King of nations invites us in our final chapter to understand how the story of God's plan in Scripture, even when focused on a single nation (Israel) and a single person (Jesus of Nazareth), has always had this universal perspective. The hope preached by the church is for all nations to come worship the one King of nations.

KING OF ISRAEL, KING OF NATIONS

One could turn to almost any page of the Bible to see a reference to God's heart for the nations, but an easy point of entry is with Abraham. The call of Abram in Gen 12 marks the beginning of God's plan of redemption for the world through the people Israel, the descendants of Abraham and Sarah. Genesis 12–50 as a whole tells the story of how God is the God of Abraham, Isaac, Jacob (renamed Israel). These ancestral narratives lay the foundation for Israel's calling in the Hebrew Bible to be God's people for the sake of the rest of the world. God's desire to use this called and chosen people to rescue the rest of the world is seen from the very beginning in Gen 12. When God calls Abraham, God promises, "I will make of you a great nation, and I will bless you, and make your name great, so that you will be a blessing. I will bless those who bless you, and the one who curses you I will curse; *and in you all of the families of the earth shall be blessed*" (Gen 12:2–3, italics added).

There are three significant elements of God's promise to Abraham in this passage. First, God promises that Abraham will become a great nation. He will have many descendants, a radical promise considering Abraham and Sarah's old age. Second, God promises that Abraham and his descendants will inherit a specific land. This will be the land of Canaan that Israel will enter after the exodus. Third, God links these first two elements to a wider purpose for the world. Abraham's calling to be a great nation with a specific land is promised for the sake of the whole world. Abraham's purpose is to fulfill God's ends for a world created by the one God and whom God has determined to rescue. A similar reiteration of this promise is found in Gen 15, where it is also joined with a covenant marked by the sign of circumcision. Covenants are a pact, or partnership, between two groups. God partners with Abraham and decides that the redemption of the whole world will be enacted through God's work with Abraham. Abraham (and the nation from his descendants, Israel) will live to be a blessing to the rest of the nations! Although it might seem strange that a God who loves all would choose to work with just one people, this election is part of a larger plan for the whole world. Israel's election was always about God's plan for the nations.

The same point is reiterated after the events of the exodus. God has recently delivered Israel from slavery in Egypt when God calls them to Mount Sinai to give them the gift of the law. Connected to this gift, God stresses that Israel's law-keeping and faithfulness is meant to be a sign for the world. As God explains, "Indeed, the whole earth is mine, but you shall be for me a priestly kingdom and a holy nation" (Exod 19:5–6). God is King of all the nations, but Israel is set apart as a priestly, holy nation to intercede for and be a light to the rest of the world. Just as a clergyperson is a set-apart member with a specific task of faithful leadership and proclamation, so Israel is a priestly nation with the task of instructing and proclaiming to the other nations. God is using the story of this particular people as a way to reach all the nations.

With this concept in mind, one can begin to understand many of the promises of the prophets about the future of the nations. As Israel grew as a nation with their land and their king, the center of their unique vocation for the world was seen in the temple in Jerusalem. The temple on Mount Zion was the *one and only* temple of the God of Israel. The other nations worshiped other gods in temples too numerous to count, but Israel insisted that there was only one God and that this God was the judge and King of all nations. There was a sense that the rest of the world had gone astray in its worship and would have to someday acknowledge the only God of Israel. They would have to learn to worship at God's only temple in Jerusalem. The prophet Isaiah could thus envision a day when the rest of the world would come to its senses and come to worship God. Isaiah proclaims, "In days to come the mountain of the LORD's house shall be established as the highest of the mountains, and shall be raised above the hills; all the nations shall stream to it" (Isa 2:2).

All of the other hills where the false gods were worshiped would be dwarfed by Mount Zion. All of the other nations would finally stream into the true temple and worship the creator God. Through Israel, all the world would be blessed and restored to their God. Similarly, Jeremiah envisioned a time when the nations would give up following their stubborn hearts and would gather in Jerusalem to worship Israel's God (Jer 3:17). This hope also seems to underlie the repeated declaration throughout the Psalms that all kings and all nations should worship the Lord God (cf. Ps 86:9; 102:15; 117:1).

The hope for the return of the nations to God became wrapped up with God's other promises to Israel about the future. When the return from exile happened and God returned, when the Messiah arose and a new law was placed on the people's hearts, the redemption of the nations would follow on its heels. Part of the beauty of "O Come, O Come Emmanuel" is that it grasps this wider story and, through the diversity of its images, presents the full constellation of Israel's hopes for the future return of God. In a similar way, the Gospels themselves use a wide array of images to make sure the readers understand the significance of Jesus' arrival. References to the salvation of the nations in the arrival of the Messiah are sprinkled throughout the stories of Jesus. John's Gospel declares that the arrival of the Messiah will be the true light that is "the light of all people" (John 1:4). Matthew uses the story of the wise men to capture the coming of the nations to bow before their true King, a foretaste of when all nations will return to the one God. The gifts of gold, frankincense, and myrrh they lay before the baby Jesus is an echo of a prophecy from Isaiah that describes the nations and kings coming from afar, who will "bring gold and frankincense, and shall proclaim the praise of the LORD" (Isa 60:9).

But perhaps the Gospel with the greatest emphasis on the return of the nations to God in Christ is Luke's Gospel. When the infant Jesus is presented in the temple, he is lifted up by the prophet Simeon, who declares "my eyes have seen your salvation, which you have prepared in the presence of *all peoples*, a light for revelation to the Gentiles and for glory to your people Israel" (Luke 1:30–32, italics added). Simeon prophesies Jesus' twofold mission. He is both the King of Israel, the king from David's line, and a light of revelation for the Gentiles. Jesus is the savior of the whole world—all people everywhere, Jew and Gentile. That same universal scope explains, at least in part, why Luke makes sure to locate Jesus' birth and ministry against the backdrop of the whole Roman Empire with his references to various historical events (e.g., the census in Luke 2:1) and historical personages (Caesar Augustus in 2:1, Emperor Tiberius in 3:1). Luke's Gospel is clear that Jesus is God's gift to the whole world. He is the King of all nations.

A similar point will be made in the Acts of the Apostles, the companion volume to Luke's Gospel. The major plot of Acts is the spread of the good news of King Jesus across the Roman Empire "in Jerusalem, in Judea and Samaria, and to the ends of the earth" (Acts 1:8). As the good news of King Jesus goes out to all the nations in Acts, people from all places flock to join Jesus' followers. The church, founded on Jesus' death and resurrection, is open to all the nations. The hopes of the Old Testament come to fruition in the spread of the gospel and the growth of the Christian community.

DESIRE OF NATIONS

But there is more to the imagery of the final verse of "O Come, O Come Emmanuel" besides Jesus' role as the King of nations. As the verse continues, we see that the King is forming a single community. He binds together all humanity into one heart and causes all the bitter divisions between them to cease. One of the most overlooked aspects of the gospel in the New Testament is the centrality of the formation of this *single* community. It is already foreshadowed for us in John 17 in Jesus' final teaching before his arrest. Jesus prays that his disciples and the believers who will follow from their preaching "may all be one. As you, Father, are in me and I am in you, may they also be in us so that the world may believe that you have sent me. The glory that you have given me I have given them, so that they may be one, as we are one" (John 17:21–22). Jesus prays that the community he is creating will be united as one, just as he is himself united to God the Father. The church is one community formed around the Messiah, just as Jesus and God the Father are one.

As the gospel spread, the believers formed a single, united community in Jesus the Messiah. Christianity quickly spread across the Roman Empire into cities throughout the Mediterranean world. It included Jews and Gentiles, slaves and free persons, the wealthy and the poor. But despite the differences between the various persons in these churches, they were taught to treat each other as brothers and sisters. They considered themselves as members of one family of God. Although there were different church communities (e.g., a church in Rome and a church in Corinth), they were all united as part of the one church in Christ. As Paul explains, "As many of you as were baptized into Christ have clothed yourselves with Christ. There is no longer Jew or Greek, there is no longer slave or free, there is no longer male and female; for all of you are one in Christ Jesus" (Gal 3:27–28). Paul here is emphatic that there ought to be one community around the Messiah, united under the single, decisive victory of Jesus' death and resurrection. There is one people of the promise to Abraham. Paul preached, prayed, and suffered to keep the Christians united despite the differences among them caused by their ethnic and cultural identities. Paul longed for the King of nations to bind the community together as one and bid the divisions cease.

Other similar longings for the unity of the Christian community are found in the New Testament. In Revelation, a vision is seen of a people of God made up of "a great multitude that no one could count, from every nation, from all tribes and peoples and languages" (Rev 7:9). Even later in Christian history, the early Christian document "The Epistle to Diognetus" notes the unity of the church despite their cultural diversity. They are all citizens of heaven, as the author explains:

> Christians are not distinguished from the rest of humanity by country, language, or custom. For nowhere do they live in cities of their own, nor do they speak some unusual dialect, nor do they practice an eccentric way of life. . . . They live in their own countries, but only as nonresidents; they participate in everything as citizens, and endure everything as foreigners. Every foreign country is

their fatherland, and every fatherland is foreign. . . . They
live on earth, but their citizenship is in heaven."[1]

The Christian vision of this single community is not a vision
of conformity without difference. The gospel was not a cookie cut-
ter meant to make every single person look identical to each another. Rather, in Christ, each person and culture, with all of their
unique beauty and distinctiveness, would nevertheless be united in
one community of faith. In modern parlance, this means that the
Americans can stay American and the Nigerians can stay Nigerian,
but they will be bound together in the single community of God.
All the nations will bring their gifts to the one God of Israel and to
Jesus, the King of nations. There is unity amidst diversity.

Unfortunately, the vision of the New Testament for a single
community—echoed by the prayer of the Advent hymn for Jesus'
defeat of our sad division—remains a future hope that we rarely
see fulfilled around us. Despite the myth of progress often heralded
in the public sphere, we are far removed from the elimination of
divisions. The destructive violence of two world wars, the ethnic
and nationalistic fighting that continues to this day, and the ongoing bigotry and racism that exist in America show how far we still
have to go. Even among Christians, practices of racism and sexism
distort the community of faith rather than proclaim the vision of
Jesus as the King of nations. Every small town in America likely
has several churches that can't stand each other and that refuse
to acknowledge that they are both part of the one community of
Christ. The same places are often filled with Christians who can't
envision sharing God's kingdom with folks from other nations. We
as a people are more likely to pray that God bless our country than
to show concern for those who are different from us. This commitment to tribe over Christ's kingdom should give us pause this
Advent season. For we serve the King of all nations, not the king of
our nation alone.

At this point, we might reconsider the significance of the
words of Hag 2:7. Haggai was a post-exilic prophet. He was active

1. "The Epistle to Diognetus," in Holmes, *Apostolic Fathers,* 700–703
(5:1–2, 5, 9).

in the restored community of Israel after their exile in Babylon. His writing is full of hope for God's coming among the people, a hope used to encourage the rebuilding of the temple. This hope for the future is reflected in Hag 2:7: "I will shake all nations, and the desire of all nations shall come: and I will fill this house with glory, saith the LORD of hosts" (KJV). Haggai imagines a future when God will return to dwell with God's people and all the nations will come to Israel to encounter the world's true God. This sounds much like the hopes seen in other prophets. What is unique, however, is this use of the term "desire of all nations." For some Christian interpreters, the "desire of nations" was a possible title for Jesus as the one whom all the nations desire. Interestingly, what the KJV translates as the coming "desire of all nations" is perhaps better translated as "the treasure of all nations" (NRSV), which is brought to the temple. In modern translations, it is not the Messiah who comes but rather the nations, who bring their treasures to God.

The debate about this translation, however, still has much to teach us. For it forges a connection between the hope in Christ as the one who reigns as the King of nations and our response as people of the nations who bring our various treasures to the one king. The unity that Christ creates as the King of nations does not result in one bland, generic people. Rather, each nation and people group is invited to bring their unique treasures, cultural identities, and gifts to Christ. The diversity of the nations is not a barrier to unity under the King of nations. It is welcomed as the greatest of gifts. Such celebration of national and cultural difference is characteristic of the earliest Christians. After all, the Christian community was originally gathered together on Pentecost by the gift of the Spirit, who allowed everyone to hear the gospel *in their own tongue* (Acts 2:1–36). Likewise, the promise of Revelation is that at the end of time, God's people will be a great, diverse multitude from every tribe, tongue, and nation (Rev 7:9).

As we approach the end of our Advent hymn, we are encouraged to expand our vision of God's church. If Christ is the King of nations, it means that all nations are welcome to come to him with their treasures. It also means that the church must continue to face the ongoing difficulties and challenges of following the Spirit in places where we will have to mend our divisions and work for unity. For us in America, this will mean repenting of the jingoism, racism, and sexism of our terrible past and moving toward a new future in Christ. If Christ is the King of nations, it will not do for us to be so consumed by our own little national interests that we overlook God's Spirit at work around the globe.

CONCLUSION

In the final verse of "O Come, O Come Emmanuel," we are challenged to see Christ as the King of nations. Emerging from Israel's unique call to be a blessing to the world, the hope for the Messiah in the Old Testament becomes wrapped up with the restoration of all nations. The hope for the universal reach of God's kingdom leaves a deep imprint on the birth of Jesus. It is greeted by wise men from afar, it is celebrated as the light of the world, and it is prophesied as the revelation for the Gentiles. In all of these ways, the coming of God in Christ is kept within Israel's story while also pointing toward the climax of the story of the whole world. Advent emerges from God's covenant with Israel, but it is always moving through Israel for the sake of creation. The church that has emerged from the arrival of the Messiah recognizes this and seeks to live as one people under the King of nations. They should welcome and invite the diversity of the nations into their community. For they see this diversity as a gift from God that brings God glory. As we celebrate Advent, may our eyes be lifted from our own small corner of the world to the praise and worship of the King of kings and Lord of lords.

DISCUSSION QUESTIONS FOR CHAPTER 7

1. What are your experiences of the church's relationship with American patriotism? What are the positive and negative aspects of this relationship?

2. Have you had an international experience with the church that has changed the way you think about the church as a global community?

3. What is the relationship of God's election of Israel to God's relationship with the rest of the world in the Old Testament?

4. How does the New Testament express Jesus' identity as the King of nations? How does this theme show up in the birth narratives of the Gospels?

5. What does a Christian unity look like that also respects the diversity of the Christian community? How does your church model this unity in diversity? What are its next steps?

6. How can your church teach Jesus as King of nations? How can this best be lived out in the specific nation in which you find yourself?

CONCLUSION

Rejoice!

As I was working on this book, I had a particularly insightful conversation with a retired clergyman and teacher over a good Southern lunch of fried chicken and mashed potatoes. When I asked how life was going, he replied by telling me of the deep sense of satisfaction he and his wife had in their retired life. They were able to do more fishing and enjoy some bluegrass concerts. They were able to travel to see family and were still able to help those around them. Whether they were traveling, reading, or repairing the ceiling fans in a widow's house, they had a deep sense of contentment in their retirement. They had found joy. Compared to many of the other retired people I know, this was startling. Often it seems that once someone is retired, they tend to stay equally as stressed and busy as when they worked. They are still dragged from place to place as if they have no control over how they spend their time. But this retired couple had arrived at a sense of joy. Notice that they did not describe themselves as happy. There is an importance difference between happiness and joy. Happiness is fleeting. It comes and goes with changes to one's circumstances. But they had joy—a deep, abiding sense of settled contentment. They knew that even if their day was interrupted by hardships or concerns, they still had an abiding sense of security.

As we come to the end of our Advent study of "O Come, O Come Emmanuel," it is only appropriate to end with a note on joy.

After all, throughout the song, the most common word is "rejoice." The whole song can be heard as a repeated command to rejoice. It might not be immediately apparent to you, but "joy" and "rejoice" are related terms. To rejoice literally means to show joy. Over and over again, the cry of the song is that we are a people who ought to rejoice. The reasons for this joy are numerous, as God has returned through Jesus in fulfillment of a range of Old Testament passages and images. Through it all, joy stands at the very heart of the Advent message and captures the major pulse of the entire season of expectation. The command to rejoice is a call for the church to take up joy.

It seems appropriate to conclude by noting several reasons that "O Come, O Come Emmanuel" invites us into rejoicing. What are some of the reasons we ought to rejoice this Advent season in light of the song's reading of the Bible? Three stand out in particular:

1. **We can have joy because God has remained faithful to God's promises throughout the story of Scripture and into the present.**

"O Come, O Come Emmanuel" presents Jesus as the fulfillment of the longings, prayers, and promises of the Old Testament. Through the song's images—from the more common language of the coming Messiah to the more obscure references to the desire of nations or the key of David—each verse reminds us that the birth of Jesus is part of a larger story that God has been orchestrating from the creation of the world. The Bible is a great narrative plotted and guided by God's steadfast love. The call to rejoice, to enter into joy, is an invitation to see that God keeps God's promises and can be trusted. There is deep security and stability, a joy that abides eternally, when we are willing to live into this great story.

2. **We can have joy because Jesus' birth, death, and resurrection have forever shaped the story of our own lives.**

The Christian proclamation of the good news takes Jesus the Messiah as its very center. It is because of Jesus' fulfillment of God's great story that we are reconciled with God. Each verse of "O Come, O Come Emmanuel" begins with Jesus, for it is in Jesus that the whole story of God's deliverance is brought to completion. He ends the exile, brings wisdom, reigns as king, welcomes the nations, frees us from our sins, and renews the whole world. Advent invites us to rejoice in who Jesus is for us and for the world. Like the colors on a patchwork quilt, each image reveals new insights into Christ's meaning for our lives. We are not left to our own devices to save and redeem ourselves. Rather, we have a firm foundation revealed by God in Jesus, giving shape and meaning to our lives and the future of the world.

We can rejoice because God has indeed come to us in Christ. Through a Son born in a manger, God has stepped down and rescued us. And because of this past story, we can rest assured that God's future will unfold as God promised. Christ will come again, the broken world will be restored, and the redeemed will be gathered into God's presence forever. As we rejoice in what the story of Jesus means for us, that same story directs our eyes to a future with God that is secure. As we celebrate the first Advent, we are promised the second Advent, the return in glory.

3. **We can have joy because the longing of the Advent season in the face of darkness and sin does not have the last word. God's story shows us that the future is secure and we are invited not to despair but to face the future unafraid.**

A major element of Advent is the longing and hope for the future of the world. The church has to acknowledge that even after the coming of Jesus, there remain elements of sin, suffering, and evil in the world. The world is not all cupcakes and rainbows. Advent occurs in the longing in the darkness, but it also looks toward the future. How is it that we can rejoice in the midst of the ever-present reality of sin, suffering, and death?

Advent reminds us that God keeps God's promises. There is a larger story at work that God has already given an ending. God has orchestrated the story from creation to the present day. And Jesus' birth, life, death, and resurrection becomes a foretaste and promise of what God has in store for the world. The victory was already won when God stepped down into creation as the Word made flesh. While we still long for this future, we can do so with an abiding joy. We are not bound to despair that there is nothing but bad days ahead. We are not bound to look at the future with anxiety, as if the future is too full of challenges for us to move. We are not bound to approach the future with apathy, as if everything is simply pointless. Instead, we are invited to face the future unafraid, to look into the future knowing that just as God was with Israel in the Old Testament and just as God came to earth as Christ, so also our own future is secure in the Messiah whom we worship.

The church's Advent rejoicing is a proclamation to the rest of the world. It is an invitation to join God's great story, to become a part of writing the final pages as we look to Jesus' return in glory. We are called to wait, pray, and work until we all see God face to face and God's glory covers the world as the waters cover the seas. Our future is decided—Christ will return in glory, and God's kingdom will come. So this Advent we declare, to ourselves and to the world, the reason for our joy:

"Rejoice, rejoice, Emmanuel shall come to you, O Israel!"

Bibliography

Holmes, Michael W., trans. *The Apostolic Fathers: Greek Texts and English Translations*. 3rd ed. Grand Rapids: Baker Academic, 2007.

Josephus. *The New Complete Works: Revised and Expanded Edition*. Translated by William Whiston. Grand Rapids: Kregel, 1999.

Meyers, Carol. *Exodus*. Cambridge: Cambridge University Press, 2005.

Peterson, Eugene. *A Long Obedience in the Same Direction: Discipleship in an Instant Society*. Downers Grove: InterVarsity, 1980.

Rutledge, Fleming. *Advent: The Once and Future Coming of Jesus Christ*. Grand Rapids: Eerdmans, 2018.

Smith, D. Moody. *John*. Abingdon New Testament Commentary. Nashville: Abingdon, 1999.

Tyson, Neil deGrasse. *Astrophysics for People in a Hurry*. New York: Norton, 2017.

The United Methodist Hymnal. Nashville: United Methodist, 1989.

Wise, Michael, et al., trans. *The Dead Sea Scrolls: A New Translation*. New York: HarperCollins, 2005.

Made in the USA
Las Vegas, NV
21 September 2024

95603316R00066